Experiential Learning and Outdoor Education

This book adds to the theoretical development of the emerging fields of experiential learning and outdoor education by examining the central concept, 'experience', and interrogating a central claim of experiential learning: whether, and if so how, a short-term singular experience can transform a participant's life as a whole and in a permanent way.

While such a possibility has been corroborated by the personal testimonies of participants, and the activities of instructors over many years, the book argues that we must go beyond this kind of 'evidence'. In comparing Anglophone and continental approaches and drawing on the work of Dewey, Dilthey and Merleau-Ponty in the philosophy of experience, *Experiential Learning and Outdoor Education* presents the first detailed review of the concept of 'experience' in European philosophy, as applied to outdoor experiential learning.

A vital insight into the field, this is important reading for students and researchers working in the philosophy of sport, and pedagogical theory, especially in areas relating to the outdoors, but also to experiential education more generally.

Jim Parry is Visiting Professor at the Faculty of Physical Education and Sport, Charles University in Prague and former Head of the Department of Philosophy, University of Leeds, UK. His main interests are in sports ethics and social and political philosophy. He is Series Co-editor of the Routledge series *Ethics and Sport*.

Pete Allison is Professor at the Pennsylvania State University, USA. His scientific interests are in experiential education, values, ethics and qualitative research. The main areas of his work are in Snowsports and the Outward Bound™ movement. He is a Fellow of the Royal Geographical Society, the Explorers Club of New York, the Young Explorers Trust and the British Exploring Society.

Experiential Learning and Outdoor Education

Traditions of Practice and Philosophical
Perspectives

Edited by Jim Parry and Pete Allison

Routledge
Taylor & Francis Group

LONDON AND NEW YORK

First published 2020 by Routledge

2 Park Square, Milton Park, Abingdon, Oxon, OX14 4RN
605 Third Avenue, New York, NY 10017

Routledge is an imprint of the Taylor and Francis Group, an informa business

First issued in paperback 2020

British Library Cataloguing-in-Publication Data
A catalogue record for this book is available from the British Library

Library of Congress Cataloging-in-Publication Data
A catalog record has been requested for this book

ISBN: 978-0-367-27929-5 (hbk)
ISBN: 978-0-367-78779-0 (pbk)

Typeset in Times New Roman
by Wearset Ltd, Boldon, Tyne and Wear

This book was written with the support of the
Grant Agency of the Czech Republic
(Grantová agentura České republiky – GAČR)
for the project
'Models of bodily experience in the theoretical foundations
of experiential education and its kinanthropological
context.'

(GAČR 16–19311S)

Contents

Notes on contributors   ix

Introduction   1
JIM PARRY

1 **Experiential pedagogy in the Czech Republic**   8
   IVO JIRÁSEK AND IVANA TURČOVÁ

2 **Experiential learning in the outdoors: the Norwegian
   tradition**   19
   HELGA SYNNEVÅG LØVOLL

3 **Influences on Anglophone approaches to outdoor
   education**   28
   PETE ALLISON

4 **Wilhelm Dilthey: lived experience and the symbolic
   productivity of the body**   37
   JIŘÍ KLOUDA

5 **Learning as differentiation of experiential schemas**   52
   JAN HALÁK

6 **John Dewey's conceptualisation of experience**   71
   JOHN QUAY

7   **The long-term influence of expeditions on people's lives**   91

MARIA-JOSE RAMIREZ, PETE ALLISON, TIM STOTT
AND AARON MARSHALL

8   **Transformative experience as a change of horizon**   112
IVO JIRÁSEK

Index   130

Contributors

Jan Halák completed a PhD in philosophy at Charles University in Prague, Czech Republic, and Université Paris 1 Panthéon-Sorbonne, France. He currently serves as Principal Investigator of a grant project supported by the Czech Science Foundation at the Department of Philosophy, Palacký University in Olomouc, Czech Republic. His project is dedicated to an interpretation of the works of Maurice Merleau-Ponty, in particular to the period of his teaching at the Collège de France. His research focuses on continental philosophy, phenomenology, ontology, embodied cognition and experiential learning.

Ivo Jirásek is Professor in Recreation and Leisure Studies and former Vice-Dean for Research (2010–2016) at the Faculty of Physical Culture, Palacký University Olomouc, Czech Republic. He specialises in philosophical aspects of movement culture (game and play, experience, body, movement), and is interested in experiential and outdoor education, and spirituality and spiritual health. He is Vice-President of the International Society for Social Sciences of Sport, and member of the executive committee of the European Association for Philosophy of Sport. He is former Editor-in-Chief of *Gymnasion, Journal for Experiential Education*, and a longtime leader at the Vacation School of Lipnice – Outward Bound Czech Republic.

Jiří Klouda is Assistant Professor at the Institute for History of Medicine and Foreign Languages of the First Faculty of Medicine, Charles University in Prague. He also works on research projects at Palacký University Olomouc and University Hradec Králové in the Czech Republic. His research focuses on continental philosophy, philosophical anthropology, philosophy of life sciences and some topics concerning ancient Greek science, philosophy and literature; and he is an experienced translator from German, Latin and Ancient Greek. Especially, he is an expert on phenomenology and *Lebensphilosophie*, and translator and interpreter of Dilthey.

Helga Synnevåg Løvoll is Associate Professor at Volda University College, Norway. She has 15 years of experience teaching *friluftsliv* and nature guiding within the three-year BA programme, including practical and academic training. Her practical interests include outdoor activities in all four seasons of the year, with a special interest in snow and glaciers. When teaching *friluftsliv*, she engages in topics such as landscape interpretations, local history, natural geography and biology. She also teaches psychology of motivation in Master and PhD Programmes. Her PhD, 'Inside the Outdoor Experience', investigates different positive emotions, categorised as hedonic versus eudaimonic feelings, and their implication for the motivational process. She is currently working on identifying the role of psychological experiences of beauty in nature.

Aaron Marshall is Chief Operating Officer at the Santa Barbara Zoo, USA. He also teaches graduate courses for Miami University, USA, at the intersection of Experiential Learning and Conservation Biology, and serves as an affiliate for the Kurt Hahn Consortium for Values and Experiential Learning, USA. Formerly a secondary educator, administrator, small business owner and Zoo Education Director, he has employed experiential learning with a values focus in a variety of contexts – including conservation learning in Belize, sail training in the Bahamas and social entrepreneurship in Cuba, Costa Rica and Uganda.

John Quay is Associate Professor in the Graduate School of Education at the University of Melbourne, Australia. His research interests include outdoor and environmental education, physical education, and philosophy of education and curriculum studies. He is also Editor of the *Journal of Outdoor and Environmental Education*.

Maria-Jose Ramirez is a PhD candidate at the Pennsylvania State University, USA. Her dissertation explores the perceived long-lasting influences of expeditions in participants' lives and the elements that fostered those influences. She also works with people whose chosen fields require high performance under pressure, including athletes and musicians. As part of her work, she develops online training programmes that help participants to reflect on their experiences, ultimately enabling them to learn what works best in their disciplines.

Tim Stott is Professor of Physical Geography and Outdoor Education at Liverpool John Moores University, UK, where he has been responsible for leading and teaching on the Outdoor Education programmes for 25 years. He has travelled widely, skiing, trekking, cycling and canoeing, and has carried out fieldwork for his research in fluvial geomorphology and outdoor education in Iceland, Svalbard, Greenland, European Alps, Australia, British Columbia, China, Peru, Bolivia and the Caucasus, as well as the UK.

Ivana Turčová is Lecturer at the Department of Outdoor Sports, Faculty of Physical Education and Sport, Charles University in Prague, where she teaches on problems of outdoor education and outdoor sports. Her doctoral studies were in 'Diversity in Language: Outdoor Terminology in the Czech Republic and the UK' (2005).

Introduction

Jim Parry

The main aim of the book *Experiential Learning and Outdoor Recreation* is to provide a comprehensive conceptual interpretation of the key issue central to the claims of advocates of 'experiential learning': whether, and if so how, a *short-term singular* experience can transform a participant's life *as a whole and in a permanent way*. While such a possibility has been corroborated by the personal testimonies of participants and the activities of instructors over many years, we must go beyond this kind of 'evidence'. The main aim of the analyses in this book is to help the disciplines of 'experiential education' and 'outdoor recreation' to move to the level of theoretical discourse.

The book aims to help experiential learning to move from a statement *that* something is happening and from a basic enumeration of *what* is happening, to an understanding and an interpretation of *how* it is happening. Only in this way will experiential learning be able to take control of the internal dynamics of the process of experiential learning; further develop in a practical way through the reflexive adoption of a systematic terminological apparatus; and have the right to claim that its essential procedures and practices are rationally embraced, reportable and theoretically grounded. In short, only in this way will it become a pedagogy in the full sense of the word.

The authors believe that in striving to fulfil these different levels of objectives, we will also be contributing to opening experiential learning to other disciplines, particularly to general pedagogy, acting as intermediaries between the general, philosophical level of the problem (the question of the structure of experience) and specific pedagogical practices.

Experiential Learning and Outdoor Education is based on the outcomes of a three-year GAČR project (Grant-awarding Czech Science Foundation Agency of the Czech Republic 2015–2018), which seeks to build a coherent philosophical base for the practice of experiential learning in the outdoors, with especial reference to Dewey, Dilthey and the phenomenological approach currently focused on Merleau-Ponty. Empirical studies are then examined in order to assess the importance that the experience retains in the long term.

These aims and objectives will be pursued in eight chapters that will examine the topic from different but complementary angles. The structure of the book is simple: the first three short chapters explore three salient outdoor education traditions, and this is followed by three original contributions to the theory of experience, and then two chapters that reflect upon the central problematic: how do we explain the fact that short-term (outdoor) learning experiences can have long-lasting (life-changing) effects?

As mentioned above, the first three short chapters investigate three important traditions in outdoor education, connecting the Anglophone tradition with practices and traditions that have received inadequate attention in English. They aim to offer insight and to consider developments in the philosophy and theory of experiential education in continental Europe, and in particular the Czech and Norwegian traditions, and to compare and contrast them with developments in Western Europe (specifically the UK). So, our first step is to present as comprehensive an account as possible of existing conceptualisations of experiential education in the outdoors, so as to provide international and complementary perspectives for the original work in the following three chapters on 'philosophy of life' (*Lebensphilosophie*) (Chapter 4), phenomenology (Chapter 5) and Dewey's philosophy (Chapter 6). This task requires a thorough review of existing literature in the field, so as to 'recover' its insights for comparison and critique. The book is completed by two chapters (Chapters 7 and 8) that address the major educational question in the field: how can a short-term experience have a long-term effect, in the radical sense of transforming a participant's life? How do we theorise the possibility of short-term Outdoor Education courses providing 'life-changing experiences'?

Chapter 1, by Ivo Jirásek and Ivana Turčová, discusses 'Experiential pedagogy in the Czech Republic'. Specific historical conditions and various political arrangements in the former Czechoslovakia – now the Czech Republic – led to a distinctive version of experiential pedagogy (*zážitková pedagogika*), which here refers to the theoretical reflection of a specific educational practice originally pursued by the Vacation School of Lipnice. This developed from movement recreation (*turistika* – active movement involving outdoor and cultural activities; the scouting movement and Jaroslav Foglar, woodcraft, and tramping) through the educational dimension of outdoor recreation (camping schools, experimental projects) to experiential pedagogy (intensive recreational regimes, Vacation School of Lipnice) and holistic education, with the method of dramaturgy as the unique contribution to the international community. The chapter starts by defining the field of experiential education and experiential pedagogy, briefly discusses its roots and development in the Czech Republic and finishes with the contemporary state of the field. The Czech approach is considered unique in the use of physical movement activities, educational, creative and gaming programmes and its holistic comprehensiveness. Dramaturgy as the main contribution of the Vacation School of Lipnice plays a key role in the Czech creative and holistic outdoor experiential programme design.

Chapter 2, by Helga Synnevåg Løvoll, discusses 'Experiential learning in the outdoors: the Norwegian tradition', in which cultural and historical heritage explain the current theory of practice, *vegledning*, as a specific version of experiential learning in Norway. This practice tradition is mostly 'lived' within educators who study *friluftsliv*, which is the Nordic term conveying how to understand outdoor life in normative ways. *Vegledning* builds on contributions by Nils Faarlund, articulated in the 1970s, as a civilisation critique where *friluftsliv* appears to be a way of 'finding home'. A core description of *vegledning* includes physical and mental preparations, quality descriptions of preferred nature areas, specific leadership styles, specific group compositions, styles of living and detailed ideas regarding how one should engage in environmental awakening. This practice tradition builds on at least three different heritages: heritage from romantic movements and national identity, heritage from Norwegian male polar heroes, and heritage from Arne Næss and the deep ecology movement.

Chapter 3, by Pete Allison, discusses 'Influences on Anglophone approaches to outdoor education' via the contribution of three influential figures in Outdoor Education, as evidenced in current practice: Jack Longland, Kurt Hahn and Surgeon George Murray Levick. Without some understanding of these three characters it is difficult to make sense of outdoor education across the UK. The unifying theme running through these three people's philosophies is that outdoor education can contribute to improving society. Longland's emphasis was on social deprivation, while Hahn and Levick were concerned with improving the individual so that they might contribute to society. Longland opened the first local education authority residential outdoor education centre, which marked the beginning of these centres across the UK in the subsequent five decades. Kurt Hahn was an educational reformer known for the creation of Outward Bound, Round Square Schools, United World Colleges and The Duke of Edinburgh Award. He is sometimes referred to as the grandfather of outdoor education. Murray Levick was an explorer who identified his own learning and, inspired by this, started the Public Schools

Exploring Society, which in turn led to the creation of a multitude of youth development expedition organisations across the UK and the world. These three individuals and their respective legacies provide insights into the foundations of current outdoor education purposes and practices in the UK.

In Chapter 4, 'Wilhelm Dilthey: Lived experience and the symbolic productivity of the body', Jiří Klouda provides an enhanced interpretation of the central notion of experience (*zážitek*). He argues that this concept can serve experiential education best, if we move to a re-understanding of the historico-philosophical context of the 'philosophy of life' (*Lebensphilosophie*) from which it emerged. The word *Erlebnis* appears in specific circumstances in German in the nineteenth century, from which it inspired other European languages, including Czech, and shaped analogous neologisms.

However, it was not until German philosopher, psychologist and historian Wilhelm Dilthey (1833–1911), that this expression was established as a new category for a new philosophical approach to a specifically human interpretation of reality, as the social sciences were being born. Dilthey is best known for his attempts to elaborate an epistemological theory appropriate to the methods used in the humanities and social sciences, and for his detailed historical studies concerning the genesis of the modern world view. This chapter focuses on a different part of Dilthey's philosophical heritage, his general inquiry into human creativity in his treatise *The Imagination of the Poet: Elements for a Poetics*. Here, Dilthey most clearly formulated his concept of 'lived experience' (*Erlebnis*). To understand this crucial notion, we must start in the first section by briefly outlining its philosophical background. The next section more thoroughly examines how Dilthey formed and utilised his concept of lived experience to describe the creative imagination that is operative in every production and perception of works of art. Third and finally, we reconsider Dilthey's aesthetic doctrine in a wider and more up-to-date context in order to show its relevance for disciplines related to purpose-free activities such as recreation, play or outdoor adventure.

In Chapter 5, 'Learning as differentiation of experiential schemas', Jan Halák aims to provide an interpretation of experiential learning that fully detaches itself from the epistemological presuppositions of empiricist and intellectualist accounts of learning. He first introduces the concept of schema as understood by Kant and then explains how it is related to the problems implied by the empiricist and intellectualist frameworks. Halák then interprets David Kolb's theory of learning that is based on the concept of learning cycle and represents an attempt to overcome the corresponding drawbacks of these frameworks. He shows that Kolb's theory fails to

achieve its goal because it is rooted in some of the fundamental epistemological presuppositions of these frameworks. Subsequently, the chapter
presents a group of works from phenomenology, in particular Merleau-
Ponty's, in order to show that Kolb's attempt is insufficient due to a lack
of understanding of the problem expressed by Kant via the concept of
schema. Finally, Halák outlines an interpretation of experiential learning
as differentiation of experiential schemas and explains how it meets the
epistemological challenges outlined above.

In Chapter 6, 'John Dewey's conceptualisation of experience', John
Quay re-interprets John Dewey's concept of experience in the context of
his works related to the problems of education (Dewey, 1938). While
many discipline-oriented discourses – for example mathematics education, science education and history education – emphasise content knowledge or pedagogical content knowledge as the major focus, outdoor
education has striven to comprehend and work educationally with the
experiences of the participants. In outdoor education, the experiences of
participants encompass both pedagogy and content. Significant among the
theorists informing such discussion is educational philosopher John
Dewey. Quay's aim in this chapter is to explore Dewey's theoretical position regarding experience and education in more detail, drawing on the
interpretation of Dewey's philosophy of education argued by another
educational philosopher, R. S. Peters (1977), in the edited book *John
Dewey Reconsidered*. Peters' positive account of the connection Dewey
makes between experience and education is of high quality. However,
Peters also takes issue with aspects of Dewey's philosophy, opening the
door to further debate. Quay provides a summarised version of Peters'
positive account and then explores his criticisms. This enables the introduction of a more coherent view of Dewey's philosophy, one that Dewey
himself struggled to clearly articulate, even though it was his aim to
express 'a coherent theory of experience'. This perspective brings
Dewey's understanding of aesthetic experience, which Peters overlooked,
into functional relation with his work in logic, or reflective experience.
Such an interpretation offers to outdoor educators a broad conceptualisation of experiential learning that may further inform various understandings of pedagogical practice.

Chapter 7, 'The long-term influence of expeditions on people's lives',
seeks to address a significant research gap in studies of outdoor experience. Although most of such research focuses on the benefit of the
experiences, the work has rarely been concerned with more than the 2–3
years after the experience. Few empirical studies are available from
which we can assess the long-term outcomes of youth expeditions. In
this chapter Maria-Jose Ramirez, Pete Allison, Tim Stott and Aaron

Marshall concentrate on the longer-term value of outdoor experiences, and the philosophical ideas surrounding the idea and possibility of 'life-changing experiences'. The chapter provides a synthesis and analysis of three very recent (and currently unpublished) studies that shed some light on the long-term outcomes for participants of three different types of youth expeditions. The three retrospective studies, in different outdoor settings, explored the perceived long-lasting influence of expeditions in participants' lives. In terms of implications for future practice, the key conclusion is that these studies confirm the importance and long-term value of such expeditions to young people and add vital evidence to the case for building such opportunities into young people's lives. Themes identified included: increased environmental awareness and appreciation of nature and the outdoors; awareness of their good fortune in having participated in an expedition; gratefulness, service and transfer to others; appreciation of leadership; and the importance of planning and preparation.

In Chapter 8, 'Transformative experience as a change of horizon', Ivo Jirásek also addresses this major educational problem – how can a short-term experience transform a participant's life? He does this by developing a philosophical model that connects the psychological theory of peak experience (Maslow) with a philosophical understanding of the phenomenological concept of 'horizon', as outlined principally in the works of Husserl and Patočka. Exceptional experiences that have the power to change human lives were first investigated in psychological and religious studies as mystical or religious experiences (James). Humanistic psychology has more recently identified such extreme, positive modes of being as peak experiences (Maslow), peak performances, peak moments or flow (Csikszentmihalyi). Although most studies have focused on these optimal events, some also accept negative experiences that have the power to transform a human life as nadir experiences or plateau experiences. This chapter will consider not only positive experiences but all experiences with transformative potential that might occasion a change of human understanding of the self, other people, nature and the world. Here, Jirásek employs the notion of horizon that comes from phenomenology (Husserl and Patočka). Experiential educators are familiar with the situation at the top of a mountain, where the horizon of what is visible changes compared with previous points of view. The phenomenological understanding of horizon accentuates this symbol as the net of all our references and meanings of what is – of what has altogether created our world. The horizon is not only the boundary of the visible part of reality but also a symbol of the world. In applying this model to experiential education courses, the transformative experience of the concrete participant can change his/her horizon and, thus, a lifelong understanding of his/her life and its meaning and relation to other people, nature, and the world.

Bibliography

Dewey, J. (1938). *Experience and education.* New York: Collier Books.
Peters, R. S. (1977). *Education and the education of teachers.* London: Routledge & Kegan Paul.

1 Experiential pedagogy in the Czech Republic

Ivo Jirásek and Ivana Turčová

Defining the field

The term 'experiential pedagogy' (a translation of the Czech concept of *zážitková pedagogika*) in the Czech Republic refers to the theoretical reflection of a specific educational practice originally pursued by the Vacation School of Lipnice – VSL[1] (Jirásek and Svoboda, 2016). For a wider context see for example Vážanský (1992), Vážanský and Smékal (1995), Neuman (2014), Jirásek (2004, 2014). This educational concept is accepted by a rather closed community that gathers people from related educational areas (adult education, drama, social education, leisure time education, etc.), in both non-formal and informal education. The concept has been developed mainly by experts from Palacký University, Faculty of Physical Culture, Department of Recreology (UP FTK) and through the specialised journal *Gymnasion*.

Researchers from Charles University, Faculty of Physical Education and Sport, Department of Outdoor Sports (UK FTVS) have been trying to find connections between the Czech tradition in 'outdoor education'[2] and new trends from abroad (turistika,[3] *pobyt v přírodě, tělocvičné aktivity v přírodě, sporty v přírodě* versus outdoor activities, outdoor education, adventure education, experiential learning) (Neuman, Turčová and Martin, 2018). Practices of 'outdoor education' vary according to culture, philosophy and local conditions (Brookes, 2006; Ford, 1986; Freakley, 1990; Lugg, 1999; Neill, 2008). The often-used terms like outdoor education, adventure education, outdoor learning, experiential learning, outdoor adventure education or adventure programming have different meanings in different countries. Neuman, Turčová and Martin (2013) concluded that the field of outdoor experiential education still suffers from cultural terminology misunderstandings. There is a need for more collaborative cross-cultural (language) research to provide greater understanding of these context-specific differences and perspectives.

The concepts of 'experiential pedagogy' and 'outdoor education' are overlapping in the Czech Republic. Educational practice is very similar, but whereas 'experiential pedagogy' is often connected with the VSL, 'outdoor education' is more associated with formal education at all levels and non-formal education of youth organisations, such as *Junák* – the Czech Scout (scouting), woodcraft, *turistika* organisations, etc.

The Czech concept of experiential pedagogy is an inspiring approach, which helps participants in different ways and through powerful learning experiences to enhance their personal development and form their own worldview. When we compare the Czech term *zážitková pedagogika* to the English 'experiential education' and the German *Erlebnispädagogik*, the English and German are more closely associated with method and philosophy, whereas the Czech approach indicates that it is a philosophical *and* pedagogical discipline. The method is related to how you proceed in your teaching, whereas pedagogy is a scientific discipline that studies education and learning as purposeful activities that form a human being.

The English term 'experience'[4] does not provide a clear specification and it is not an easy term to define, as it often implies contradictory meanings (Fox, 2008; Jay, 2005). Different meanings in relation to the field of experiential education are distinguished by Roberts (2008): experience as an interaction (based on Dewey's pragmatism) and embodied experience as praxis (inspired by critical theory). The field of experiential education is then perceived as a method of education, which includes three types of relationships: with oneself, with others and with the natural environment (Proudman, 1992; Quay, 2013). Inconsistency in terminology (in using the term 'experience') is also discussed in the literature by Becker, Braun and Schirp (2007), Becker (2016), Breuning (2005), Fox (2008) and Payne (2002).

Roots and sources of experiential pedagogy

The Czech form of experiential pedagogy and experiential courses were constituted by the following principal ideas.

Turistika, *stays in nature*

The indigenous nature of Czech *turistika*[5] activities (active ways of travelling aimed at exploring natural as well as cultural phenomena) have attracted recent attention in international outdoor literature (see Martin, Turčová and Neuman, 2016; Neuman, Turčová and Martin, 2018). Foundations of *turistika* activities were laid in the book *Turistický katechismus* (Guth-Jarkovský, 2003), who stated that *turistika* could be a sport, but its aim is not only the development of physical fitness, since it also contributes to aesthetic and educational experience. The main aim is learning about nature and about experiences gained in nature, and this feature can be found in *turistika* activities even today. *Turistika* activities have been developed through the *Turistický* club, the *Sokol* movement (a physical education organisation) and *Junák* (scouting), which have continued to develop during periods of oppression, and have provided opportunities to preserve Czech culture and language. *Turistika* as an active movement (on foot, bike, skis, canoe or horseback) is considered as a leisure activity with an educational dimension. It has always been a part of physical education. *Turistika* in its various forms was earmarked as a special form of staying in nature in addition to outdoor sports on the one hand and recreation on the other hand (in addition to camping, games, mushrooming or fishing). From a conceptual perspective it is clear that *turistika* brings experiences in various modes, for example adventure or risk (Neuman *et al.*, 2000). *Turistika* activities are also one of the core programme parts delivered by the VSL.

The scouting movement

The world scouting movement was transformed into Czech scouting (*Junák – the Czech Scout*[6]) by A. B. Svojsík, who mixed together aspects of British scouting and American woodcraft, placed it into the mild Czech landscape, full of forests, meadows, streams and rivers, and adjusted it to Czech culture. His book *Základy Junáctví* (*The Foundations of Scouting*), published in 1912 (Svojsík, 1912), is a key work. In this book Svojsík used the term 'outdoor education' for the first time in Czech literature.

   Junák has made a significant contribution to the formation of positive values for young people in the Czech Republic. It is currently the largest youth organisation[7] that spends time outdoors with children and young people. After 1989 it also added and adapted some experiences from the VSL into its programmes for young people. In the past *Junák* put great emphasis on learning skills and knowledge. However, today, Czech scouts have moved towards developing more practical skills, involving problem-solving tasks and team work. Typical activities include games and competitions during weekdays (club and group meetings in clubrooms), at weekends (expeditions in nature) and on holidays camps. Summer camps (over 1,000 annually) are an important culmination of their whole-year work. Scouting encourages children and youth towards self-education.

Jaroslav Foglar

Jaroslav Foglar, the scout, writer, educator and editor of magazines, influenced the experience of hundreds of scout members and also thousands of young people through reading clubs in the magazines *Mladý hlasatel* and *Vpřed* (Pírek, 1990). His legacy includes a typical emphasis on mystique, mystery and romance, but also an impulse for the transformation of education into self-education. Foglar's principles of boyhood are risk-taking, active life, honest behaviour and learning in nature with others in a small group. His values and educational principles and methods include a healthy lifestyle, an interest in nature, honourable behaviour, group cohesion and a holistic approach. Foglar's specific outdoor adventure characteristics include timelessness, place (landscape), romance, mystery and challenge, and traditions with rituals (Jirásek and Turčová, 2017). All these features are included in the phenomenon of play in all its forms, and this has become the symbol of the Czech form of experiential pedagogy. But it is also the motivational power of the legend that is used in presenting a programme and inducing an enticing atmosphere. Part of the legacy is also the difficulty of the programme, which requires all-out effort, competitiveness, measuring one's skills, the use of language for an adventurous active programme, etc.

Woodcraft

Inspired by American woodcraft and E. T. Seton, Czechs also developed their own Czech form of woodcraft – The League of Forest Wisdom (*Liga lesní moudrosti*). The books and ideas of E. T. Seton and his Woodcraft Indians were translated and adjusted for the Czech context by another secondary school teacher of natural science, translator and writer Miloš Seifert (Seifert, 1920). Woodcraft is still alive today[8] in the Czech Republic and focuses on leading a simple life in nature. This movement influenced summer camps by promoting understanding of the beauty of nature, the camp fire, staying in nature in basic Indian teepees, and interest in the native people from different parts of the world, especially North America, in the ways of their rituals, songs, clothing and games. Woodcraft encourages sustainable relationships to nature and the value-based education of young people (Seton, 1991). The system of personal development is shaped by moral principles of the symbolism of the quadruple fire (beauty, truth, love, power) and is organised by means of tests to win eagle feathers.

Tramping

The Czech tramping tradition (Hurikán, 1990) can be described as an unorganised, free-thinking movement, realised by weekend escapes from the cities into nature, and into tramping settlements. It has developed a specific subculture in opposition to consumerist society. Tramping developed its own culture, slang, songs, clothes, flag, anthem, rituals, magazines, literature, sports and small settlements (i.e. cottage colonies). These special settlements with wooden cabins and simple places for camping with a campfire were built in beautiful natural environments especially near rivers around Prague and other bigger towns.

The educational dimension of outdoor recreation

In the 1960s and 1970s, leisure time began to be perceived not only as a form of relaxation and entertainment, but also as a space for personal development (Teplý, 1969). Since the 1970s the educational discourse of understanding leisure time activities, including stays in nature, has strengthened. Outdoor educators started to look for so-called 'modern' forms of outdoor education.

Camping schools

Successful elements in scouting and woodcraft entered *Pionýr*[9] more and more in the early 1960s and a search for new forms and programme components led to so-called *Tábornické školy* (camp schools). Camp schools (Snopek, 1969; Stárek, 1974) used experiences of former scouts, tramps and woodcrafters and were inspired by traditional forms of Czech outdoor stays. The essential aspects were not only the programme components and the environment, but also purpose, including personal and ideological influences. Leaders and instructors were mainly people from banned organisations and teachers from UK FTVS. Camp schools later inspired the foundation of the VSL, which was supposed to promote new forms of outdoor stay for the Czechoslovak youth.

Experimental projects and intensive recreational regimes

Experimental projects were the direct predecessor of VSL. Their influence was to link physical education and cultural activities. A true legend was the project called *Gymnasion* attempting to explore new forms of stays in nature and outdoor education (Neuman and Hanuš, 2007). The frequently pronounced mottos of that time were action, intensity, atmosphere, a search for new elements and, most importantly, a strong educational interest. 'The aim is to change activity in nature to *outdoor education*' (Smékal, 1986, 362). The emphasis was on play for adults, and its symbolic dimension, or its differentiation from entertainment (Gintel, 1973).

'Intensive recreational regimes'[10] is another name for the same movement at that time, which included challenging content into its programmes. The focus on the age group of younger adolescence distinguishes these educational efforts from other concepts and systems.

Vacation School of Lipnice

In 1977 the VSL was founded under the Social Youth Union as an outcome of seminars dedicated to experimental forms of stays in nature and outdoor education. The study by Neuman and Hanuš (2007) shows the significant contribution of VSL to the development of outdoor education and adventure education programmes up to 2000. VSL's focus and activity, and also the theoretical background for its activity, have changed over the years. During the course of nearly four decades, various courses and other activities have developed. Many members of VSL and the Department of Outdoor Sports (UK FTVS) had already started to become interested in adventure education before 1989, and had realised several expeditions abroad (e.g. to Russia by Lake Bajkal).

After 1989 VSL focused on outdoor education. VSL staff also integrated problem-solving games, ropes courses, etc., and visits to Outward Bound Schools (in the UK and New Zealand) resulted in programme reviews and the joining of Outward Bound International in 1992. Safety standards began to be discussed more and applied in practice. Foreign instructors helped at courses and seminars, which initiated further theoretical explanation of the work and programmes at VSL.

In 1999 Outward Bound Czech Republic became a commercial organisation under the name Outward Bound – the Czech Way (*Česká Cesta*). It connected the Czech concept of VSL with the traditional approaches of Outward Bound. It also focuses on outdoor training, outdoor management development and City Bound courses. However, it has recently separated formally from Outward Bound International, and they no longer use the logo nor the words 'Outward Bound' in their name (see: https://ceskacesta. cz/). However, the VSL is still a member of Outward Bound.

Today VSL is a not-for-profit civic organisation. It focuses on experiential pedagogy and youth development. It promotes a holistic approach to outdoor experiential education and it stresses 'dramaturgy', placing a great emphasis on creative course design, and its facilitation and reviewing. Their aim is to form a balanced relationship between people, society and nature. They deliberately work with 'experiences' and carefully choose programme elements with the potential to have maximum influence on course participants' development. Using a dramaturgy approach to course design, they organically join outdoor activities, games and physically demanding activities with psychological games, art and drama activities.

The courses are traditionally residential (in the VSL outdoor centre), expeditionary or combined, summer or winter, aimed at developing managerial skills, creativity, social issues, methodological aspects, for students of secondary schools or universities, adults, seniors, parents or grandparents with children.

Experiential pedagogy

In the 1990s in the Czech Republic there appeared the terms 'education of experience' (Vážanský, 1992) and 'education through experience' (Neuman, Vomáčko and Vomáčková, 1999). At the beginning of the millennium the theoretical concept of experiential pedagogy had been formed, initially influenced by German Erlebnispädagogik, and later, in 2002, it formed its own theoretical framework, published by Jirásek (2004). Later he suggested that practical activities should be defined as 'holistic education', while theoretical reflections (methodological research-based) should be identified as experiential pedagogy:

> The Czech approach, combining holistic education with method of dramaturgy, is considered unique and differs from foreign concepts (outdoor education, adventure education, experiential education) in the use of physical movement activities with educational, creative and gaming programmes. The Czech form of projects grouped under experiential pedagogy exceeds the dimensions of individual definitions through its holistic comprehensiveness and can be seen as a unique Czech contribution to international community. Experiential pedagogy focuses mainly on younger adolescents, and only then on other age groups.

'Dramaturgy' can be perceived today as one of the main contributions of VSL to the educational area (Hanuš and Chytilová, 2009; Hora, 1984; Holec, 1994; Martin, Franc and Zounková, 2004; Martin, Leberman and Neill, 2002). Dramaturgy is a process that not only helps to structure individual programmes into a scenario with their maximum possible exploitation – it is also primarily the constitution of the whole project, i.e. considering and selecting the ideas of the production team. The purpose of this process is to select specific programme parts, but also their correct timing. 'It is not important what activities are included in the programme but what objectives are followed' (Gintel, 1982, 7). Intentions, goals and conceptions are always the centre of attention, and are followed by the structure of individual programme components and the principles of their arrangement (Gintel, Gregor and Čepeláková, 1986). The term 'dramaturgy' plays a key role in Czech creative and holistic outdoor experiential programme design, involving physical movement activities, original games, art, music and drama activities, social and group problem-solving activities, psychological and reflective activities.

To read more on the Czech way, see Martin, Franc and Zounková (2004), Martin, Turčová and Neuman (2016) or the most recent chapter by Neuman, Turčová and Martin (2018).

Notes

1 *VSL (Prázdninová škola Lipnice – PŠL)* is a not-for-profit civic organisation and a member of Outward Bound International focusing on experiential pedagogy (*zážitková pedagogika*) and youth development. Instructors deliberately work with 'experiences' and carefully choose programme elements with the potential to maximally influence course participants' development. Using a dramaturgy approach to course design, they organically join outdoor activities, games and physically demanding activities with psychological games, art and drama activities.

2 The term 'outdoor education' is used quite broadly to refer to a range of organised activities that take place in predominantly outdoor environments for a variety of purposes (Neill, 2008).

3 Turistika is 'active movement involving outdoor and cultural activities' (see Neuman, Turčová and Martin, 2018).

4 The Czech language has three different terms: *prožitek* – experience (I), *zážitek* – experience (II) and *zkušenost* – experience (III). The difference is in the sense of temporality. Experience (I) is the present experience, an intense way of living, characterised by non-transferability. Experience (II) refers to past experiencing and experience (III) is the processed experience, which is transferable.

5 The Czech term *turistika* should be distinguished from the word tourism (a tourist spends more than 24 hours in a different place or a country for a reason that is not related to his work – e.g. learning, recreation, etc.). The Czech language does not have words that would distinguish active movement from tourism. In English we can find words such as trekking, hiking, walking or rambling. For active forms of travelling the German language uses the word *wandern* (*fusswandern* – on foot, *skiwandern* – on skis, *radwandern* – on a bicycle, *bergwandern* – in the mountains). However, in these countries it is rather an activity aimed at finishing a certain journey, reaching a certain distance and choosing the right equipment. The learning activity is not stressed, as it is in *turistika*.

6 The name of the Czech scouting organisation.

7 It registers over 50,000 children, youth and adult volunteers in more than 1,600 youth and 400 adult groups.

8 It registers some 50 tribes with more than 1,000 members organising 30 summer camps annually.

9 Pionýr is a youth organisation founded in the 1970s under the strong influence of the socialist regime with the aim to direct the free time of children and youth, and to promote communist ideas.

10   The word 'recreational' means that this period shall be used to restore physical and mental strength. The word 'intensive' means that the arrangement of the 'regime' of activities includes activating stimuli and situations, whose mere experiencing is insufficient, the participants must also act.

(Smékal, 1986, 358)

Bibliography

Becker, P. 2016. From 'Erlebnis' to adventure: A view on the German Erlebnispädagogik. *In:* Humberstone, B., Prince, H. and Henderson, K. A. (eds) *Routledge international handbook of outdoor studies*, London, Routledge.

Becker, P., Braun, K. H. and Schirp, J. (eds). 2007. *Abenteuer, Erlebnisse und die Pädagogik*, Opladen, Verlag Barbara Budrich.

Breuning, M. 2005. Turning experiential education and critical pedagogy: Theory into practice. *Journal of Experiential Education*, 28, 106–122.

Brookes, A. R. 2006. *Situationist outdoor education in the country of lost children*, Australia, Melbourne, Deakin University.

Ford, P. 1986. Outdoor education: Definition and philosophy. *Eric Digest.*

Fox, K. 2008. Rethinking experience: What do we mean by this word 'experience'? *Journal of Experiential Education*, 31, 36–54.

Freakley, M. 1990. *Understanding outdoor education: A case of subject definition.* Unpublished master thesis. University of Queensland, Australia, Brisbane.

Gintel, A. 1973. Gymnasion: část první – vážná, avšak podstatná. *Metodické listy pro pobyt v přírodě*, 3, 2–4.

Gintel, A. 1982. Obrana vůdčích myšlenek aneb dramaturgie. *Metodické listy pro tělovýchovně brannou činnost*, 10, 7–9.

Gintel, A., Gregor, J. and Čepeláková, J. 1986. Dramaturgie aktivních rekreačních systémů [Studijní texty Instruktorského kursu PŠ SSM]. Unpublished text.

Guth-Jarkovský, J. S. 2003. *Turistika: turistický katechismus*, Praha, Baset.

Hanuš, R. and Chytilová, L. 2009. *Zážitkově pedagogické učení*, Praha, Grada.

Holec, O. 1994. *Instruktorský slabikář*, Praha, Prázdninová škola Lipnice.

Hora, P. 1984. *Prázdniny se šlehačkou: malá instruktorská čítanka, inspiromat pro chvíle bezradnosti*, Praha, Mladá fronta.

Hurikán, B. 1990. *Dějiny trampingu*, Praha, Novinář.

Jay, M. 2005. *Songs of experience: Modern American and European variations on a universal theme*, Berkeley, University of California Press.

Jirásek, I. 2004. Vymezení pojmu 'zážitková pedagogika'. *Gymnasion: časopis pro zážitkovou pedagogiku*, 1, 6–16.

Jirásek, I. 2014. Inzerát na název. *Gymnasion: časopis pro zážitkovou pedagogiku*, 8, 11–19.

Jirásek, I. and Svoboda, J. 2016. *Non-religious peregrination and meaning of life: Transformation of human being in winter nature*, Saarbrücken, Germany, Scholars' Press.

Jirásek, I. and Turčová, I. 2017. The Czech approach to outdoor adventure and experiential education: The influence of Jaroslav Foglar's work. *Journal of Adventure Education and Outdoor Learning*, 17, 321–337.

Lugg, A. 1999. Directions in Outdoor Education curriculum. *Australian Journal of Outdoor Education*, 4, 25–32.

Martin, A., Franc, D. and Zounková, D. 2004. *Outdoor and experiential learning: An holistic and creative approach to programme design*, Aldershot, Gower Publishing.

Martin, A., Leberman, S. and Neill, J. 2002. Dramaturgy as a method for experiential program design. *Journal of Experiential Education*, 25, 196–206.

Martin, A. J., Turčová, I. and Neuman, J. 2016. Turistika activities and games, dramaturgy and the Czech outdoor experience. *In:* Humberstone, B., Prince, H. and Henderson, K. A. (eds) *Routledge international handbook of outdoor studies*, London, Routledge.

Neill, J. 2008. *Enhancing life effectiveness: The impact of outdoor education programs*. Unpublished doctoral thesis. University of Western Sydney, Australia, Sydney.

Neuman, J. 2014. Koncepce 'zážitkové pedagogiky' – přínosy i kritické pohledy. *Gymnasion*, 8, 20–28.

Neuman, J. and Hanuš, R. 2007. Kristova léta školy prázdninového času. *Gymnasion: časopis pro zážitkovou pedagogiku*, 4, 17–55.

Neuman, J., Brtník, J., Šafránek, J., Vomáčko, S. and Vomáčková, S. 2000. *Turistika a sporty v přírodě: přehled základních znalostí a dovedností pro výchovu v přírodě*, Praha, Portál.

Neuman, J., Turčová, I. and Martin, A. J. 2013. Czech research in outdoor experiential education. *Journal of Outdoor Activities*, 7, 74–79.

Neuman, J., Turčová, I. and Martin, A. J. 2018. Education in nature programmes in the Czech Republic since 1989. *In:* Becker, P., Loynes, C., Humberstone, B. and Schirp, J. (eds) *The changing world of the outdoors. European reflexions*, London and New York, Routledge.

Neuman, J., Vomáčko, L. and Vomáčková, S. 1999. *Překážkové dráhy, lezecké stěny a výchova prožitkem*, Praha, Portál.

Payne, P. 2002. On the construction, deconstruction and reconstruction of experience in 'critical' Outdoor Education. *Australian Journal of Outdoor Education*, 6, 4–11.

Piaget, J. 1952. *The origins of intelligence in children*, New York, W.W. Norton & Co.

Pírek, Z. 1990. *Čtenářské kluby Jaroslava Foglara*, Brno, Delfín.

Proudman, B. 1992. Experiential education as emotionally-engaged learning. *Journal of Experiential Education*, 15, 19–23.

Quay, J. 2013. More than relations between self, others and nature: Outdoor education and aesthetic experience. *Journal of Adventure Education and Outdoor Learning*, 13, 142–157.

18   *Ivo Jirásek and Ivana Turčová*

Roberts, J. 2008. From experience to neo-experiential education: Variations on a theme. *Journal of Experiential Education*, 31, 19–35.

Seifert, M. 1920. *Přírodou a životem k čistému lidství: příručka českých junáků*, Praha, Dědictví Komenského.

Seton, E. T. 1991. Kniha lesní moudrosti (M. Zapletal, Trans. 2nd edn. Original edition, 1921), Praha, Olympia (The Book of Woodcraft).

Smékal, V. 1986. Výchova a pobyt v přírodě. *Teorie a praxe tělesné výchovy*, 34, 358–362.

Snopek, V. 1969. *Tábornická škola*, Praha, Mladá fronta.

Stárek, M. 1974. Tábornické školy jak byly, jak jsou a jak by měly být. *Metodické listy pro pobyt v přírodě a turistiku*, 4, 15.

Svojsík, A. B. 1912. *Základy junáctví: návod pro výchovu čes. skauta na zákl. systému R. Baden-Powella Scouting*, Praha, J. Springer.

Teplý, Z. 1969. *Pohybová rekreace*, Praha, Universita Karlova.

Vážanský, M. 1992. *Volný čas a pedagogika zážitku*, Brno, Masarykova Univerzita.

Vážanský, M. and Smékal, V. 1995. *Základy pedagogiky volného času*, Brno, Paido.

2 Experiential learning in the outdoors

The Norwegian tradition

Helga Synnevåg Løvoll

Introduction

Norwegian *friluftsliv* is a way of experiencing nature for the sole enjoyment of being immersed among nature. In the Norwegian language, *friluftsliv* defines both a phenomenon (Bischoff, 2012; Gelter, 2000, 2010) and specific discourses of meaning (Tordsson, 2003). The term differs from the straightforward translation of 'outdoor life' by interpreting certain qualities within the experience associated with philosophic meaning (Gelter, 2010; Henderson and Vikander, 2007; Varley and Semple, 2015). *Friluftsliv* also refers to pedagogical practice, as it often appears within course names or studies as well as physical education curricula. *Friluftsliv* may be considered a facet of experiential learning, but the latter is much wider than *friluftsliv* alone. In this presentation, we will focus on how *friluftsliv* is presented as pedagogic practice.

Defining the field

There are at least three different approaches for understanding modern practices of *friluftsliv*: pedagogy *for friluftsliv*, pedagogy *with friluftsliv* and pedagogy *within friluftsliv*.

Pedagogy for *friluftsliv*

Friluftsliv pedagogic practices, as they appear in K-12 schools, camp schools and higher education, are inspired by environmental thinking in the 1970s. Nils Faarlund (1974) raised the classical work of pedagogy for *friluftsliv*: '*vegledning*', defined as a theory of practice for *friluftsliv*. The term generally translates to 'supervision' or 'conveyance', but there is ambiguity as to whether the term is spelled '*vegledning*' or '*veiledning*'. *Vegledning* is highly value-oriented and understated by a word introduced by Faarlund, while *veiledning* literally translates as 'supervision'. The core ideal of pedagogy revolves around the act of learning by experience and reflection. A main principle is deciding both route and activity based on participants' competence (Faarlund, 1974). Mastering skills needed for the chosen activity is an absolute necessity. Thus, it is more efficient to begin with easy tasks and then progress towards complex ones, much like approaching steep terrain. Although there have been some disagreements on *vegledning* as a new term in Norwegian language, the preferred approach of teaching *friluftsliv* based on competence levels of participants has maintained strongly resonant among *friluftsliv* educators[1] (Horgen, 2009; Magnussen and Vold, 2018; Mytting and Bischoff, 2007; Tordsson, 1993).

Pedagogy with *friluftsliv*

In the mid-1990s, experiential learning emerged as 'outdoor school' within Norwegian primary schools (Jordet, 2010). This pedagogical practice focuses on the benefits of learning 'social outdoor practice' (Jordet, 2010). Within arguments for moving learning processes outside the classroom, the international field of experiential learning is generally inspired by Dewey, Kolb and Vygotsky, among additional scholars (Jordet, 1998, 2007, 2010). The term '*Uteskole*' refers to the outdoor and nearby interpretation of pedagogical approaches to nature, which are not necessarily considered phenomena or specific meanings:

Outdoor school is a way to work with the school's content on where students and teachers use the nearby area and local communities as a resource in education – to supplement and complement classroom education. Uteskole involves regular and targeted activity outside the classroom (Jordet, 2010).

This relatively new tradition includes a variety of practical, aesthetic and creative approaches to learning, including interdisciplinarity (Fiskum and Husby, 2014), use of play, role-play and dramaturgic approaches (Buaas, 2002; Kjelen, 2015). For pupils with special needs, *friluftsliv* contributes significantly towards 'social learning' (Sølvik, 2013).

Pedagogy within *friluftsliv*

In this approach, there is a 'within' perspective of different explorations of engagement in nature, including deeper meanings of *friluftsliv*. For example, experiences involving landscapes are bodily experiences that influence our cultural and social interpretations relative to a specific place (Krogh, 1995). Different groups have experienced the same landscape in different ways; these experiences are entirely dependent upon cultural constructions (Gurholt, 2000). The frames of hiking – i.e. choosing between an old path to the summer farm or a newly-designed dirt road within the same landscape – has a tremendous influence on bodily experience and interpretation of meaning (Bischoff, 2012). When observing everyday practices of *friluftsliv*, people experience obstacles and limitations in their approach to nearby forests that connect to general changes in society (Skår, 2010). Children learn by exploring nearby nature areas, using their imagination to fabricate and play inside their own fiction worlds (Fasting, 2012).

The relevance of physical challenge in children's play is important, where development of learning is highly related to their environments (Sandseter, 2010). This perception is also deepened in adult kayaking experiences, in which many find 'playscapes' in high waves (Magnussen, 2011). *Friluftsliv* includes a richness of positive emotions, where hedonic and eudaimonic emotions seem to play different roles in the motivational process (Løvoll, 2016; Vittersø, 1998). Ethnographic studies of emotions also identify struggles between emotional belonging and social death among minority youths studying Norwegian culture (Broch, 2018).

While many approaches to experiential learning may possess similarities regarding general engagement with nature, the most special Norwegian contribution is most likely the tradition built after the 1970s, when *friluftsliv* was established in higher education. The theory of practice, identified as *vegledning*, builds on at least three roots of cultural heritages.

Heritage from romantic movements and national identity

Nature plays an important role in Norwegian individuals' perception of culture and health (Regjeringen, 2015–2016). While nature surely defines Norwegians' identities today, this cultural trait can be interpreted as a continuous history, beginning with Edda poetry and continuing through the Viking era, romantic literature of the nineteenth century, Ibsen poetry that introduces *friluftsliv* (Ibsen, 1871) and the Eco philosophical movement inspired by Arne Næss (Witoszek, 1998). Nature has defined Norwegians for centuries. Moreover, nature has been available along with the Norwegian public's right to free access in uncultivated land (Reusch, 2012); many families have access to summer farms due to late urbanisation and the continuous use of mountains for harvesting.

Inspired by romantic movements of the late nineteenth century, Norwegian nature is central to cultural expression in art (i.e. Tidemand and Gude), literature (i.e. Ibsen and Vinje) and music (i.e. Grieg); additionally, a new interest in mountaineering is arising for the sake of mountaineering itself, as opposed to obligations, exclusively, of everyday life. Thomas Heftye established a tourism association in 1868 in an attempt to make nature more available (Maske, 2017). Cabins and huts appeared, and routes marked with small stone cairns became established. Soon, several local associations appeared all over Norway. In 1985, all local associations unified into one association, and they agreed on the aim 'to encourage the simple *friluftliv* for a broader audience', including children and adolescents. In 2017, the total number of members passed 300,000, and this number is continuing to increase.

While the first hikers and mountaineers belonged to the upper middle class, mountains were generally a place for equality and class liberty; the doctor was encouraged to engage in small talk with the farmer, against the costumes within cities (Gurholt, 2000; Richardson, 1994). In the 1930s, *friluftsliv* appeared as an arena for building a social democratic nation, symbolising liberty and social equality, and typically illustrated by social democratic Norwegian ministers Sunday-hiking in nearby Oslo forests (Tordsson, 2003).

Heritage from Norwegian male polar heroes

In the late nineteenth century, Fritjof Nansen became a legendary hero and key symbol of the dawning, independent Norwegian identity (Gurholt, 2008). His genuine interest in science and adventure guided him towards several polar expeditions, in which he crossed the Greenland ice cap in 1888 and became the first individual to discover the North Pole's geographical location during a three-year expedition from 1893–1896. Nansen was also a famous speaker and writer during his time (e.g. Nansen, 1926/1961) and received the Nobel Peace Prize in 1922 for his work involving victims following the First World War. Although he was a charismatic individual, there were many myths circulating about his personality that supported the image of 'virile men'; this image was, coincidentally, partly built by Nansen himself (Gurholt, 2008).

Nansen has been a great inspirator concerning the timeless articulation and value of *friluftsliv* (Repp, 2001, 2007). Moral virtues, such as adventurousness, playfulness, connectedness to nature and civilisation critique, are personified through Nansen and are executed through values of *friluftsliv*. Taking a critical perspective, it can be argued that modern *friluftsliv* education is a reproduction of adventure as a male domain, where core values of the initial articulations of *friluftsliv* might be overlooked (Gurholt, 2008).

Heritage from Arne Næss and the deep ecology movement

During the green wave of the 1970s, Arne Næss was a notable inspirator of environmental awakening in Norway. The professor of philosophy quit his position at the University of Oslo in 1970 in order to engage in efforts against the ecology crisis full-time and contribute to philosophical arguments through what he calls deep ecology (as opposed to shallow and technology-optimistic ecology) (Næss, 1976).

Næss introduces his definition of *friluftsliv* as 'more or less playful forms of short stays in nature' (Næss, 1976, p. 303). Moreover, he argues that today's forms of *friluftsliv* are characterised by losses in modern urban lifestyles. In order to reduce these losses, life has to change into patterns of green politics by living in local communities with rich access to varied nature, using both soft and close technology. *Friluftsliv* based on responsibility includes showing respect for all life and landscapes, promoting deep and rich experiences while simultaneously reducing competition and focusing on goal achievements, minimising one's ecological footprint, maximising self-sufficiency, practicing a natural lifestyle with minimal implementation of technology and devoting plenty of time towards one's own peace, serenity, and silence (Næss, 1976).

Vegledning – *what, why and how*

Inspired by values from the deep ecologic movement, *friluftsliv* appears as a political arena where nature consciousness and the cultivation of positive emotions towards nature is absolutely central. Within these aims, a certain theory of practice was developed (Faarlund, 1974). The learning cycle consists of preparations, reflections and experiences both during hikes and after work/reflection. The chosen area is very significant as it incorporates wilderness qualities without the need for too much travelling.

The preferred working style involves organising small, heterogenic groups of participants, where three to seven participants seem to be optimal. There is a focus on basic skills that include knowledge of clothing, nutrition, cooking, navigation, safety, assembling a campsite, etc. In an ideal situation, group members learn from each other, with each member contributing various knowledge and experiences. If the group succeeds in self-organising itself, the leader can observe the group without being too disruptive of the group process. If the group does not succeed, its members will require stronger leadership, in which case the leader must participate more enthusiastically and/or mandate clearer instructions (Tordsson, 1993).

The learning cycle follows classical patterns of experiential learning; in the morning there is a meeting in which the entire day is planned;

discussions are held concerning weather, health issues and possible difficulties within the preferred plan (Faarlund, 2015). During a hike/activity, the gold standard is to give room for each individual's own development by trying and succeeding or trying and failing, so long as safety is maintained. If this process goes well, the most important role of the *vegleder* is to inspire nature consciousness by telling stories about the place, interpreting qualities in the landscape and promoting revelations about deep ecology. If the group is not well managed, the *vegleder* needs to choose a stronger leadership role in order to keep the group safe during activities. In rainy and/or stormy weather, the *vegleder* might prefer the guide-role for the purpose of creating safer experiences for participants. Therefore, the *vegleder* must be sensitive to the group's needs and safety by practicing 'situation-based leadership'.

In the evening, the group gathers to discuss the day's experiences. This discussion is part of the learning process, where the *vegleder* attempts to develop interpretations of experiences into nature consciousness; the vegleder is expected to have 'something' important to say. Participation with *vegledning* include organisation from early morning to late evening. In this tradition, the playfulness is present, but it follows some unwritten rules: spontaneous tree- and rock-climbing qualifies as 'yes', while ski jumping qualifies as 'no'. Activities containing competitive elements take the focus away from the nature and experience.

During a seminar for educators of *friluftsliv*, led by Nils Faarlund in 1979, several agreements arose concerning best practices of *vegledning* (Magnussen and Vold, 2018, pp. 126–127).

a   The situation: qualities of 'free nature'.
b   Group size: small groups.
c   Group composition: heterogeneity.
d   Duration: several days are necessary to dwell.
e   Style of living: being part of both the group and nature.
f   Equipment, clothes, and food: thinking/acting safely, being a role model.

Recently, Magnussen and Vold (2018) supplemented the practical approach by including four principles in *their* theory of practice: (1) Deciding route and activity after participant's competence, (2) Leave no traces, (3) Participation and responsibility: be prepared and informed, and (4) Activity-based learning: focus on learning activity rather than the leadership.

Today, a *vegleder* is not a protected title. There have been some attempts to describe the professional roles in which guiding has regulations informed by the tourism industry, while the *vegleder* does not (Andersen and Rolland, 2016). *Vegledning* is a topic covered in half-year courses as well as three-year Bachelor programmes. While the empiric tradition is currently developing some approaches to *friluftsliv*, the field suffers from having a short academic history as far as the description of the full theory of practice. Dwelling on the roots of *vegledning*, there are valid reasons for questioning myths about national heroes as well as core values of *friluftsliv*. The aim is to develop a consistent and holistic approach for how to teach *friluftsliv* as the most desirable practice possible.

Note

1 Although there are disagreements over the notion of 'vegledning' (some favouring 'veiledning') the notion ... etc.

Bibliography

Andersen, S. and Rolland, C. (2016) 'Naturguiding – profesjonalisering eller kommersialisering av friluftslivskompetanse?' in Horgen, A., Fasting, M. L., Lundhaug, T., *et al.* (eds) *UTE: Friluftsliv – pedagogiske, historiske og sosiologiske perspektiver*. Oslo: Fagbokforlaget.

Bischoff, A. (2012) *Between me and the other, there are paths ... A PhD thesis on paths, people and the experience for nature*. PhD: Norwegian University of Life Sciences.

Broch, T. M. (2018) *Equilibrium Poems: An ethnographic study on how experiences in and with Norwegian friluftsliv challenge and nurture youths' emotion work in everyday life*. PhD: Norwegian School of Sport Sciences.

Buaas, E. H. (2002) *Med himmelen som tak: om uterommet som inspirasjonkilde og verksted*. Oslo: Universitetsforlaget.

Faarlund, N. (1974) *Friluftsliv: hva – hvorfor – hvordan*. Hemsedal: Høyfjellsskolen norsk alpincenter.

Faarlund, N. (2015) *Friluftsliv*. Oslo: Ljå forlag.

Fasting, M. L. (2012) *Vi leker ute: en fenomenomlogisk hermeneutisk tilnærming til barns lek og lekesteder ute*. PhD: NTNU.

Fiskum, T. A. and Husby, J. A. (2014) *Uteskoledidaktikk. Ta fagene med ut*. Oslo: Cappelen Damm Akademisk.

Gelter, H. (2000) '*Friluftsliv*: The Scandinavian philosophy of outdoor life', *Canadian Journal of Environmental Education*, 5, pp. 77–92.

Gelter, H. (2010) '*Friluftsliv* as slow and peak experiences in the transmodern society', *Norwegian Journal of Friluftsliv*, 1, pp. 1–22.

Gurholt, K. (2008) 'Norwegian friluftsliv and ideals of becoming an "educated man"', *Journal of Adventure Education and Outdoor Learning*, 8, pp. 55–70.

Gurholt, K. (2000) '*Det har bare vært naturlig': Friluftsliv, kjønn og kulturelle brytninger*. PhD: Norwegian School of Sport Sciences.

Henderson, B. and Vikander, N. (2007) *Nature first: Outdoor life the Frilufsliv way.* Toronto: Natural Heritage Books.

Horgen, A. (2009) *Friluftslivsveiledning vinterstid.* Oslo: Cappelen Damm.

Ibsen, H. (1871) *Digte.* København: Forlagt af den Gyldendalske Boghandel (F. Hegel). Thieles bogtrykkeri.

Jordet, A. N. (1998) *Nærmiljøet som klasserom: uteskole i teori og praksis.* Oslo: Cappelen akademisk forlag.

Jordet, A. N. (2007) *'Nærmiljøet som klasserom': en undersøkelse om uteskolens didaktikk i et danningsteoretisk og erfaringspedagogisk perspektiv.* no. 80. Det utdanningsvitenskapelige fakultet: Universitetet i Oslo.

Jordet, A. N. (2010) *Klasserommet utenfor.* Oslo: Cappelen Akademisk Forlag.

Kjelen, H. (2015) *Det utvidede læringsrommet.* Oslo: Fagbokforlaget.

Krogh, E. (1995) *Landskapets fenomenologi.* PhD: Norges Landbrukshøyskole.

Løvoll, H. S. (2016) *Inside the outdoor experience: On the distinction between pleasant and interesting feelings and their implication in the motivational process.* PhD: University of Bergen.

Magnussen, L. I. (2011) 'Play – the making of deep outdoor experiences', *Journal of Adventure Education and Outdoor Learning,* 12, pp. 25–39.

Magnussen, L. I. and Vold, T. (2018) *Friluftsliv og guiding i natur. Teori og praksis.* Oslo: Universitetsforlaget.

Maske, J. (2017) 'Fra elite til folkebevelgelse' in Maske, J. (ed.) *Historien. DNT Årbok.* Oslo: Den Norske Turistforening.

Mytting, I. and Bischoff, A. (2007) *Friluftsliv.* Oslo: Gyldendal.

Nansen, F. (1926/1961). 'Eventyrlyst' in Nansenskolen (ed.) *Speech on St. Andrew's University.* Oslo: Norsk Humanistisk Akademi.

Næss, A. (1976) *Økologi, samfunn og livsstil: utkast til en økosofi.* Oslo: Universitetsforlaget.

Regjeringen. (2015–2016) 'Meld. St. 18. Friluftsliv – natur som kilde til helse og livskvalitet' in Miljødepartementet, K.-O. (ed.). Oslo: Regjeringen.

Repp, G. (2001) *Verdiar og ideal for dagens friluftsliv: Nansen som føredøme?: tankar og formuleringar om friluftslivet i vår tid: spegling av Nansen sine verdiar og ideal?: ei samanliknande gransking.* Institutt for samfunnsfag: Norges idrettshøgskole.

Repp, G. (2007) 'How modern Friluftsliv started: Fridtjof Nansen, instigator and model' in Henderson, H. and Vikander, N. (eds) *Nature first.* Toronto: Natural Heritage Books.

Reusch, M. (2012) *Allemannsretten – friluftslivets rettsgrunnlag.* PhD: University of Oslo.

Richardson, H. (1994) *Kraftanstrengelse og ensomhet. En analyse av det norske friluftslivets kulturelle konstruksjoner.* Master: University of Oslo.

Sandseter, E. B. H. (2010) *Scaryfunny. A qualitative study of risky play among pre-school children.* PhD: NTNU.

Skår, M. (2010) *Experiencing nature in everyday life.* PhD: Norwegian University of Life Sciences.

Sølvik, R. M. (2013) *Friluftsliv som sosialt læringslandskap for ungdom i risiko. Eit fenomenologisk-inspirert kasusstudium.* PhD: University of Oslo.

Tordsson, B. (1993) *Perspektiv på friluftslivets pedagogik.* Bø i Telemark: Telemark distriktshøgskole.

Tordsson, B. (2003) *Å svare på naturens åpne tiltale: en undersøkelse av meningsdimensjoner i norsk friluftsliv på 1900-tallet og en drøftelse av friluftsliv som sosiokulturelt fenomen.* PhD: Norwegian School of Sport Sciences.

Varley, P. and Semple, T. (2015) 'Nordic slow adventure: Explorations in time and nature', *Scandinavian Journal of Hospitality and Tourism*, 15, pp. 73–90.

Vittersø, J. (1998) *Happy people and wonderful experiences. Structure and predictors of subjective well-being.* PhD: University of Oslo.

Witoszek, N. (1998) *Norske naturmytologier: fra Edda til økofilosofi.* Oslo: Pax Forlag.

3 Influences on Anglophone approaches to outdoor education

Pete Allison

Three notable characters have influenced outdoor education in the UK – Jack Longland, Kurt Hahn and Surgeon George Murray Levick. Understanding these three characters provides insights that help to make sense of outdoor education across the UK. The unifying theme running through these three people's philosophies is that outdoor education can contribute to improving society. For Longland the emphasis was on social deprivation while for Hahn and Levick they were concerned with improving the individual so that they could contribute to society (very similar to John Dewey's philosophy of education).

Murray Levick was an explorer who identified his own learning (primarily on the *Terra Nova* expedition) and, inspired by this, started the Public Schools Exploring Society (PSES), which in turn led to the creation of a multitude of youth development expedition organisations across the UK and the world. Kurt Hahn was an educational reformer known for the creation of Outward Bound, Round Square Schools, United World Colleges and The Duke of Edinburgh Award. He also played a role in inspiring what is now known as Sail Training International. His contribution to a range of education and youth development opportunities means that he is sometimes referred to as 'the grandfather' of outdoor education. Longland opened the first local education authority residential outdoor education centre, which initiated the development of these centres across the UK in the subsequent five decades.

These three individuals and their respective legacies provide insights into the foundations of current outdoor education purposes and practices in the UK.

Surgeon George Murray Levick (1876–1956)

Perhaps the least well known of the three people discussed in this chapter, Levick led a life of significant adventure. Following the famous 1910–1913

Expedition to Antarctica with Captain Scott he returned to the UK to serve in both the First and Second World Wars. For this chapter the main focus will be on his experiences in Antarctica as the antecedents to his vision for personal development through expeditions. Immediately after completing medical school, aged 26, he joined the Navy, where he met a colleague who was a member of Shackleton's *Nimrod* Antarctic expedition. In 1910 Levick joined Scott on the Terra Nova expedition to Antarctica, returning in 1913. During the sail to Antarctica Scott commented on Levick in his journal as follows:

> I am told that he has some knowledge of his profession, but there it ends. He seems quite incapable of learning anything fresh. Left alone, I verily believe he would do nothing from sheer lack of initiative ... I am afraid there is little to be expected of him.

Little did Scott know how wrong he could be and, unfortunately, did not survive to see the error of his judgement. During the expedition Levick and five others known as the Northern party survived remarkable hardship including six months living in a snowhole, sleeping on stones and seaweed, and consuming only seal and penguin meat. When spring finally came they undertook a 230-mile, ten-day journey pulling sledges to get back to the main base, where they learned of the deaths of Scott and his four colleagues on their return from the pole. During the whole expedition various research projects were undertaken – Levick focusing on penguin observations and on nutrition. The hardships are difficult to comprehend, and the details are fascinating, but space does not permit them to be recounted here in detail. Interested readers are encouraged to read Guly (2016) and Lambert (2001).

On his return from Antarctica in 1913 Levick served in the Navy throughout the First World War, and then worked in London specialising in rehabilitation (mostly of veterans) and working with the blind. In 1932, as a result of his experiences specifically on the *Terra Nova* expedition, he took a group of boys from Grammar Schools on an expedition to Lapland and started the Public Schools Exploring Society (PSES), which later became the British Schools Exploring Society (BSES) and is now known as the British Exploring Society (BES).

Expeditions have continued each year (with the exception of 1939–1944) to all continents, focusing on jungles, arctic, high altitude and desert wilderness environments. Perhaps not surprisingly, given his experiences in Antarctica, the PSES focused on personal development through science and adventure, which continues to be the hallmark of these expeditions to this day.

In the context of this chapter and book, the story of Levick is important, as this provided the spark for subsequent 'youth development through expeditions' organisations later to be established, such as Brathay Exploration Group (1947), The Yorkshire Schools Exploring Society (1964) and Operation Drake/Raleigh (1978). During the 1980s and 1990s a proliferation of similar organisations (charities and for-profit) evolved to create a significant sector of outdoor education provision in the UK. Most participants in youth expeditions are either at school or university, and many are undertaking a 'gap year' between the two; and an increasing number are from a wider range of socio-economic backgrounds. Readers interested in learning more about this area of provision in the UK might read Allison, Stott, Felter and Beames (2011).

Kurt Hahn (1886–1974)

Hahn was born in Berlin to Jewish parents and studied philosophy at various universities, although never completed a degree. Towards the end of the First World War he served as private secretary to Prince Max of Baden, with whom he subsequently co-founded Salem School in Bavaria. This proved to be an important time, when Hahn developed his ideas. During the Second World War Hahn was translating and interpreting British media, and no doubt was party to top secret information at the highest level.

Subsequently, he articulated his concerns as 'decays':

1   The decay of fitness due to our modern methods of locomotion
2   The decay of self-discipline helped by stimulants and tranquilisers
3   The decay of enterprise due to the widespread disease of *spectatoritis*
4   The decay of skill and care helped by the decline in craftsmanship
5   Above all the decay of compassion which [Archbishop] William Temple called spiritual death.

(Hahn, 1958, p. 4)

The presentation of issues in this style is an indication of at least two things: (a) Hahn's concern with society, social issues and the importance of individuals coming to understand their role in contributing to civic society; and (b) Hahn's ability to phrase things in a politically appealing manner which tends to rally allies to a cause. This second point is important in understanding Hahn as a politically astute educational reformer, which is an often overlooked feature of his life, to be discussed further below.

Hahn's approach to addressing these decays was to provide the following as part of young people's education, also known as the seven laws of Salem:

1 Give children the opportunity for self-discovery.
2 Make the children meet with triumph and defeat.
3 Give the children the opportunity of self-effacement in the common cause.
4 Provide periods of silence.
5 Train the imagination.
6 Make games important but not predominant.
7 Free the sons of the wealthy and powerful from the enervating sense of privilege.

In 1933 Hahn wrote to the alumni of Salem and advised that they had to be either for Salem or Hitler but could not support both. No doubt he knew the risks of such an act and not surprisingly he was imprisoned by Hitler as a result. With the help of colleagues at Oxford (where he had previously studied) and the British Prime Minister (Ramsay MacDonald) he was released and moved to the UK where he started Gordonstoun School in 1934 (and was naturalised as a British citizen two years later). One feature often overlooked in this story is that Hahn was clearly well connected – he was of the upper classes, and such achievements and opportunities should be understood in this context.

Hahn had studied philosophy and many of his educational ideas can be connected to Plato, in particular *The Republic*. One interesting feature of Hahn's legacy is that he wrote very little beyond speeches, sermons and meeting minutes. James (1990) has described studying Hahn's life as akin to studying a 'moving spirit'. Learning about Hahn's life, it is clear that he had a sense of urgency and some impatience – perhaps because he had some awareness of the horrific events that were possible and later became a reality in the Second World War. Hahn was primarily concerned with making people, and therefore societies, more compassionate.

Outward Bound is perhaps one of the most famous organisations that Hahn co-founded with Lawrence Holt in 1941. Interestingly, Hahn was almost entirely absent from reports of events during the first three years of operation (1941–1944), while Holt was more involved with regular meetings with the warden (Jim Hogan). During that time Hahn was focused on influencing the work of the Norwood Committee that informed the 1944 Education Act – to this day the most important legislation for education in the UK. This is further confirmation that Hahn was first and foremost interested in education reform and saw politics as a crucial route to achieve it.

Hahn subsequently inspired the foundation of The Duke of Edinburgh Award (a badge scheme which he had developed originally at Gordonstoun), United World Colleges and Round Square Schools – all of which continue to flourish today and operate in keeping with Hahn's overall vision and philosophy. Consistent with Hahn's belief in the importance of service as a means of moving from relationships based on pity for others to compassion for others, all of these organisations continue to incorporate ongoing service to other human beings as a critical pillar of practice.

Regardless of agreement, or otherwise, with Hahnian philosophy (of which there are many interpretations) it is undeniable that he has had an enormous influence on outdoor education practices across the globe and specifically in the UK. Hahn has influenced practices in Outward Bound schools, which are charitable organisations, but also in residential outdoor centres such as those inspired by Longland. Further, his philosophy continues also to influence public schools such as Atlantic College in Wales. Readers interested in Hahn's life are advised to read his original work, James (1990), Veevers and Allison (2011) and Allison (2016).

Jack Longland (1905–1993)

Longland attended Jesus College Cambridge where his interest in climbing was sparked by a community of explorers and climbers including Geoffrey Winthrop Young and Gino Watkins. In 1933 he went on the British Expedition to Everest and in 1935 to East Greenland. He became a lecturer at Durham University in English Literature and developed growing concerns for the welfare of unemployed people, which was evident in the area at that time, given high unemployment from local coalfields in the late 1920s and early 1930s. His increasing interest in social conditions and in disparities between the South and North of England led him to leave Durham University in 1936 to begin work in the management and leadership of education, and in community service, for the rest of his career. His esteem as a climber, public speaker and educational leader brought him numerous roles, including chairman of the Mountain Leadership Training Board (1964–1980), but he is perhaps best known in outdoor education circles for starting the first Local Education Authority (LEA) outdoor pursuits centre in 1950 – White Hall – in the Peak District National Park.

At the opening of White Hall centre there was no clear statement regarding purpose but the detailed historical investigations by McDonald (2018, pp. 193–194) indicate the following to be a reasonable summary:

> the provision of basic training in hillcraft in all weathers and in the allied sports of climbing, caving, camping, canoeing and ski-ing

wherever conditions are suitable; to set before those coming to the Centre a vision of greatness in Nature and in Man, to inspire them with it and to persuade them to approach it in humility. This involves the training of self-reliance, the discipline of living together, the opportunity for the boy and girl to use their abundant physical and nervous energies in activities which can do nothing but good. It involves an uplifting of the spirit and a challenge to the whole personality. It provides natural penalties, sharper than a referee's whistle, for inefficiency, slackness and selfishness. All these advantages can be gained without overtaxing strength, providing the work is continuously adjusted to the age and condition of the student and to the weather.

Embedded in the above quote is a narrative regarding the benefits to the individual of spending time in the outdoors and the residential experience at the new centre. This might now be understood as contributing to what is sometimes referred to as Personal Social and Health Education (PSHE) or Social Emotional and Ethical Learning (SEEL).

Following the opening of White Hall numerous outdoor centres were opened by different LEAs across the UK – some purpose built but many in converted buildings/large houses. All of these centres were based on something similar to these ideas and created opportunities for young people to experience residential outdoor education as part of their education regardless of their social class or ability to pay. How well connected to the curriculum in school these experiences were, is another question. In some cases the school curriculum was almost seamless in preparatory work and post residential work across multiple subject areas but especially physical education and geography. In other cases the residential week was treated more as a break from the rhythm of school and curricular connections were limited. These issues are further explored by Thorburn and Allison (2010, 2013, 2017).

One further notable legacy of Longland is that he believed in equal opportunities for boys and girls and made a conscious effort to ensure balanced numbers of each participating in activities at White Hall from the beginning. He was very explicit in writing about 'boys and girls' or 'young men and young women', which subsequently became the 'norm'. For comparison, PSES (founded by Levick and discussed above) first accepted girls on expedition in 1980, which was at that time considered to be progressive. Longland was committed to opportunities for boys and girls 30 years earlier.

Many LEA outdoor centres thrived in the 1970s and 1980s but in the 1990s the Conservative government ('the Thatcher years') is often blamed for the decline of funding and associated closure of many centres. In addition, in 1993 the high-profile Lyme Bay tragedy which led to the Young Persons Safety Act in 1995 may have impacted provision and, in particular, willingness of teachers to take young people to residential outdoor centres (Allison and Telford, 2005).

As an established and respected mountaineer and educational leader there are many reasons to admire and respect the accomplishments of Jack Longland. His commitment to alleviating poverty and providing opportunities for young people to mature into responsible members of society through residential outdoor education centres is a legacy to be held in high regard. Those interested in Longland and White Hall are encouraged to read McDonald (2018).

Themes and practices

The summaries of the philosophies and practices of these three notable characters highlight pertinent aspects of their lives and their underpinning beliefs and philosophies as they relate to outdoor education. Over time their philosophies have become more intertwined as residential centre staff go on expeditions and work in public schools. This cross-fertilisation of philosophies and practices through the years means it is increasingly difficult to trace antecedents and there are other notable characters who are in the shadows here: individuals such as Drasdo (1972/1998, 1997) and Mortlock (1984) are worthy of note; and Baden Powell, the founder of the scouting movement and a significant influence on youth development through the outdoors. History is in an ongoing state of creation and recreation of narratives, and others have influenced practices and organisations over the years – both within these three traditions (expeditions, public schools, Outward Bound, badge schemes and residential centres) and in other traditions. Interested readers are directed to Smith and Knapp (2011), which is an invaluable resource.

The three individuals taking the limelight in this chapter are but a subset of those who have influenced outdoor education in the UK. It will be useful to undertake further rigorous work to highlight contributions of women, cross-cultural and peacebuilding programmes, work in mainstream schools and work done in parallel to these highlighted individuals in other countries – Norway and the Czech Republic in particular. Work examining the crossover of many of the influential individuals might provide insights regarding collaborations, friendships, competition or disagreements, interactions and exchanges between others detailed elsewhere in this book.

In the UK, outdoor education was seen as an extension of the Physical Education (PE) curriculum at White Hall, and this historical connection can be seen today in many schools where outdoor education is 'housed' within the PE department. It remains to be seen whether outdoor centres can sustain themselves with decreasing levels of funding from education authorities or whether market forces will dominate and result in an increasingly mixed provision in terms of costs, opportunities, purposes and quality. This is a place where Outward Bound have become more involved over a long period with provision for schools. In addition, Outward Bound have, in various countries, extended their provision and purpose to serve different social needs in society, incorporating peacebuilding, and drawing on work such as Lederach (2005). Expeditions for young people have expanded beyond Levick's original vision, with some organisations incorporating community service (connecting to Hahn's vision) in addition to, or instead of, the science originally envisioned by Levick.

As further investigations shine the spotlight of inquiry on certain blind spots of history, insights and depth will be added to the understanding of current practice of outdoor education. The foundations of the philosophy of outdoor education as a moral enterprise established and built upon by Levick, Hahn and Longland remains of current and, no doubt, future importance.

Bibliography

Allison, P. R. (2016). Kurt Hahn. In Joy A. Palmer Cooper (Ed.), *Encyclopedia of Educational Thinkers* (pp. 4). London: Routledge.

Allison, P. R. and Telford, J. (2005). Turbulent times: Outdoor education in Great Britain 1993–2003. *Australian Journal of Outdoor Education, 9*(2), 21–30.

Allison, P. R., Stott, T., Felter, J. and Beames, S. (2011). Overseas youth expeditions. In M. Berry and C. Hodgson (Eds), *Adventure Education: An Introduction* (pp. 187–205). London: Routledge.

Drasdo, H. (1972/1998). *Education and the Mountain Centres*. Penrith: Adventure Education.

Drasdo, H. (1997). *The Ordinary Route*. Glasgow: The Ernest Press.

Guly, H. R. (2016). George Murray Levick (1876–1956), Antarctic explorer. *Journal of Medical Biography, 24*(1), 4–10.

Hahn, K. (1958). Address at the forty-eighth annual dinner of the old centralians. *The Central: The Journal of Old Centralians, 119*, 3–8. Retrieved 22 June 2019, from www.kurthahn.org/wp-content/uploads/2017/02/2017-oldcentral.pdf.

James, T. (1990). Kurt Hahn and the aims of education. *Journal of Experiential Education, 13*(1), 6–13.

Lambert, K. (2001). *The Longest Winter: The Incredible Survival of Captain Scott's Lost Party*. Washington, DC: Smithsonian Books.

Lederach, J. P. (2005). *The Moral Imagination*. Oxford: Oxford University Press.

McDonald, P. (2018). *The Story of White Hall Centre: Outdoor Education across the Decades*. New Zealand: Otago.

Mortlock, C. (1984). *The Adventure Alternative*. Milnthorpe: Cicerone Press.

Smith, T. and Knapp, C. (Eds) (2011). *Sourcebook of Experiential Education: Key Thinkers and Their Contributions*. London: Routledge.

Thorburn, M. and Allison, P. R. (2010). Are we ready to go outdoors now? The prospects for outdoor education during a period of curriculum renewal in Scotland. *The Curriculum Journal, 21*(1), 97–108.

Thorburn, M. and Allison, P. R. (2013). Analysing attempts to support outdoor learning in Scottish schools. *Journal of Curriculum Studies, 45*(3), 418–440.

Thorburn, M. and Allison, P. R. (2017). Learning outdoors and living well? Conceptual prospects for enhancing curriculum planning and pedagogical practices. *Cambridge Journal of Education, 47*(1), 103–115.

Veevers, N. and Allison, P. R. (2011). *Kurt Hahn: Inspirational, Visionary, Outdoor and Experiential Educator*. Rotterdam: Sense.

4 Wilhelm Dilthey

Lived experience and the symbolic productivity of the body

Jiří Klouda

German philosopher, psychologist and historian Wilhelm Dilthey (1833–1911) is best known for his attempts to elaborate an epistemological theory appropriate to the methods used in the humanities and social sciences, and for his detailed historical studies concerning the genesis of the modern worldview. This chapter focuses on a different part of Dilthey's philosophical heritage, which stood apart from his principal methodological writings, although it was closely connected with them. It is in his treatise *The Imagination of the Poet: Elements for a* Poetics,[1] which is a general inquiry into human creativity, that Dilthey most clearly formulated his concept of 'lived experience' (*Erlebnis*). To understand this crucial notion, we must start in the first section by briefly outlining its philosophical background. The next section more thoroughly examines how Dilthey formed and utilised his concept of lived experience to describe the creative imagination that is operative in every production and perception of works of art. Third and finally, we reconsider Dilthey's aesthetic doctrine in a wider and more up-to-date context in order to show its relevance for disciplines related to purpose-free activities such as recreation, play or outdoor adventure.

Dilthey's philosophy of life – between philosophy of consciousness and philosophical anthropology

Let us start with perhaps the most quoted lines from Dilthey's writings. At the beginning of the first book of his voluminous and unfinished *Introduction to the Human Sciences* (1883), he programmatically declared:

> No real blood flows in the veins of the knowing subject constructed by Locke, Hume, and Kant, but rather the diluted extract of reason as a mere activity of thought. A historical as well a psychological approach to the whole human being led me to explain even knowledge

and its concepts ... in terms of the manifold powers of a being that wills, feels, and thinks; and I do this despite the fact that knowledge seems to be woven of concepts derived from the mere contents of perception, representation, and thought. Therefore, I will use the following method in this book: I will relate every component of contemporary scientific thought to the whole of human nature.

(Dilthey, 1989, pp. 50–51)

As we can see, Dilthey defines his philosophical position in contrast to the Western tradition of philosophy of consciousness. He claims that the modern philosophical tradition in its empiricist as well as aprioristic forms largely neglects other than cognitive ways in which the human being communicates with the world. According to Dilthey, our connection with reality involves cognition (perception and thinking), feelings and volition. Human nature as a whole is constituted by these human faculties only if taken together, since each of them is, to some extent, always active in every mental act. Common language distinguishes thought from volition and volition from feeling, and this is for good reason, because in each concrete act one of the faculties usually predominates. From the theoretical point of view, however, we need to pay attention to those particular situations in which the three capacities reveal themselves as fundamental, because mutually irreducible. According to idealistic aesthetics, for example, aesthetic delight should be thought of as the purest form of feeling, which does not contain any desire, and therefore does not lead to any action. In contrast to that, other types of feelings or affects, such as fear, usually do lead to some action. Aesthetic feeling mobilises our will only to focus our attention on a purely beautiful aesthetic object. As is evident, however, this is a particular case of a general structure that leads us to conclude that feelings are mixtures of emotional and volitional moments.

Dilthey's philosophical goal to relate human knowledge to human nature as a whole brought him to a new model of consciousness. In agreement with the previous mainstream Western tradition, he considers consciousness as the only 'place' where humans can meet themselves and their world. In the unpublished *Draft* for second volume of the *Introduction* he writes:

My consciousness is the locus which encompasses this seemingly immeasurable external world; it is the stuff from which the objects that press on one another are woven.

(Dilthey, 1989, p. 245)

Dilthey must, however, enlarge the traditional model of consciousness, so it also includes emotional and volitional acts. Consciousness conceived in accordance with 'the whole of human nature' acquires some important features that enable Dilthey to avoid some well-known difficulties typical in particular for the continental philosophical tradition. Dilthey was clear about the fact that the hidden predominance of the cognitive attitude, in which the representing mind (subject) and the represented thing (object) are sharply distinguished, significantly distorts our picture of reality. One of the radical consequences of this distortion is phenomenalism, the paradoxical opinion that the world exists only as my idea. When Dilthey attempted to formulate the new model of consciousness as the place where things appear to us (i.e. become phenomena), so as to avoid the consequences of phenomenalism, he carried out a pioneering phenomenological inquiry into the nature of feelings.

The classification of types of feeling will be important for the structure of Dilthey's *Poetics*, but it also has a general philosophical importance. Most importantly, simple feelings do not allow us to distinguish subject and object in them (unlike in perceptual or thought representations). We only feel an 'I', and this 'I' is not discernible from the feeling. The 'I' that feels finds itself in such and such a mood and cannot be separated from the momentary feeling. (Of course, we can reflect on our feelings, but this is not the act of feeling itself.)

Feelings and volitions connect us with the reality in a more intimate way than a reflexive cognition. However, a feeling does not completely lack cognitive value, because in feelings we immediately find ourselves in our momentary mood. Dilthey also considers another important aspect of feeling: an emotional act, despite its immediate and, so to say, intimate nature, does not completely exclude the dimensions that we usually consider as something external or objective.

First of all, we must acknowledge that feelings have a social dimension. There are particular types of feelings connecting us to our social environment, such as the family, religious community or nation. Shared emotions constitute people's belonging to the same community. And on the opposite side of the spectrum of sociality, we evidence feelings founded in the body, for example the 'general feeling' indicating our physical condition (Dilthey, 1985, p. 79, 1997, p. 195), or other types of feeling connected to sensations. These feelings are never neutral – they reveal our situation as being positive or negative, which is why they serve as the origin of action. This aspect of feelings is of crucial importance. A feeling is 'nothing merely subjective, as the traditional opinion maintains' (Dilthey, 1997, p. 110); rather, it is a unity of a situation and our attitude to it, an interconnection of the subjective and the objective.

The traditional philosophy of consciousness interprets subjectivity primarily on the basis of its cognitive capacities. Now, Dilthey was able to overcome the worst difficulties of this philosophy by developing his phenomenology of feelings. For example, if we conceive of the mind as a solipsistic, private sphere or a spirit, any attempt to connect it to the body ultimately leads to unnatural and enigmatic constructions. Consciousness as conceived by Dilthey is, however, of a completely different nature. As Dilthey explained in his *Introduction to the Human Sciences*, he aimed at elucidating how 'the whole of human nature' conditions different varieties of knowledge.[2]

For instance, our free will participates in the constitution of things, because we experience them as something *independent*, as 'something in itself'. Dilthey himself unfortunately did not provide a comprehensive account of consciousness interpreted in this way. More important for us, however, is the fact that in different parts of the *Introduction* we find the words 'lived experience' (*Erlebnis*).[3] The expression is not used here as a part of a fixed terminology, it is not explicitly defined, but the passages in question (e.g. Dilthey, 1989, pp. 330; 340) clearly suggest that 'lived experience' has to be understood as a particular type of experience related to our feelings and volition and making it possible for us to be rooted in reality.

Dilthey had good reasons to introduce *Erlebnis* as a new philosophical term. His aim was to avoid the traditional metaphysical notion of being, because he thought that it had been strongly influenced by the predominance of the cognitive attitude and subject–object metaphysics, similar to the way in which our concept of experience was influenced by certain procedures characteristic of early modern Galilean and Cartesian science. Strictly speaking, we cannot say 'I am' or 'I exist', if this statement involves an understanding of the self as an entity separated from the world and frontally facing the world. Dilthey sometimes excessively uses the terms such as 'life', 'lived experience' and similar, because he attempts to find a more appropriate terminology to express our human way of being: we can say neither that a human *exists* nor that it *is*. Rather, humans *live*. Life, according to Dilthey, is a persistent dynamic exchange or circulation between a person and his or her natural and social environment.

The concept of lived experience and its function in Dilthey's *Poetics*

Before we comment on the concept of lived experience developed in his treatise on poetic imagination, we need to discuss Dilthey's ideas regarding the task and nature of this discipline. In his *Poetics*, Dilthey deals with problems of literature, art and aesthetics in general. As we might expect, his understanding of art does not depend on some metaphysical standard of beauty, but on the other hand, he does not intend to deny the existence of all principles either. His poetics aims to establish an elementary common ground, on which authors, readers, and critics could think about and evaluate works of (literary) art. The only place where Dilthey can find these normative principles is in consciousness, as he considers it in his anthropology:

> At first, poetics had a firm basis in a classical model from which it abstracted, then later in some kind of a metaphysical concept of the beautiful. Now poetics must seek this firm basis in the life of the psyche.
>
> (Dilthey, 1985, p. 54)

By asking how we can unite a normative claim and the historically conditioned nature of every theory of art, Dilthey's *Poetics* returns to the central topics of the unfinished *Introduction to the Human Sciences*. As we will see later more in detail, Dilthey successfully advanced in his inquiry because he abandoned the narrow epistemological focus of the *Introduction*. In order to explain the exceptional and striking nature of human consciousness, 'the life of psyche', he had to create a basic psychological (today we would rather say 'anthropological' or 'phenomenological') terminology, distinct from the concept of a mechanical association of ideas that was prevalent in the psychology of the eighteenth and nineteenth centuries.

An important notion in his new terminology is the 'psychic continuum' or 'nexus of psychic life' (cf. Dilthey, 1985, pp. 71–73). The 'life of the psyche' is, according to Dilthey, an unceasing process, which constitutes the most profound foundation of the experience of time. The second meaning of continuum relates to Dilthey's psychological principle, according to which there are no fixed elements in the psychic life, neither simple sensual perceptions nor abstract ideas serving as absolutely solid 'atoms' (in the sense of the physics of the nineteenth century) in the stream of consciousness. Yet by denying the existence of firm psychical atoms, Dilthey does not defend the idea that there is nothing to be discerned in the psyche.

The psychic continuum functions as a structure or 'Gestalt' founding the difference between centre and periphery, midpoint and horizon. What is just appearing in the centre of this structure is constituted in its content and meaning by the periphery. So for example it is impossible to remember exactly a perceived image if, between the perception and the recollection, something else has captured our attention: the structure of the psychic continuum has been transformed in the meantime, so the recollected image does not completely correspond to the perception (although the difference is usually negligible).

In this way, the continuum regulates each particular set of contents and assures coherence between them in the stream of psychic life. It rules not only our thoughts and perception, but also our emotional and conative acts. This continuum is, according to Dilthey, 'acquired', because every individual builds it during his or her lifetime. As a structure connecting the 'I' and the world, the psychic continuum forms itself in an individual and personal way. This does not mean, however, that it is something subjective and solely private. It involves also supra-individual systems such as languages or established customs, and it is formed by events of both personal and social context and history. It is the dynamic unity of psychic structure, where the somatic, existential, socio-cultural and historical dimensions of human life grow together.

To sum up, and to put it in more philosophical terms, the structure of the psychic continuum is empirical and *a priori* at once: it unites what just appears and the conditions of possibility of this appearance. In other words, lived experience is the kind of experience that significantly changes the conditions of all subsequent experiences. This claim is true in general, but Dilthey asks how the acquired continuum of psychic life functions more concretely. He focuses on lived experience as a substantial part of poetical work:

> The real nucleus of poetry, lived experience, contains a relation of the inner and the outer. 'Spirit and garment,' animation and embodiment, the significance of a sequence of shapes or sounds, and the visual image for an ephemeral psychic state – an artist sees these relations everywhere.
>
> (Dilthey, 1985, p. 158)

Accordingly, lived experience can have one of these two basic forms: it is 'either something inner that manifests itself through something outer or an external image that is enlivened by something inner' (ibid., p. 117). What does Dilthey mean by 'the outer' and 'the inner'? The outer, the images, as we have seen above, are all sensorially perceptible structures of content, and events (they are visible, audible, tactile and so on). The inner aspect is more difficult to describe properly, because it only manifests itself through the outer aspect. It is possible to define it in a simplified way as a 'psychic state', as Dilthey sometimes writes, although he also acknowledges that this way of speaking is in fact questionable, because it conceptually divides what should remain dissolutely united:

lived experience, which forms the essential content of all literature, always involves a state of mind as something inner and an image or a nexus of images, a place, situation, or person as something outer. The living power of poetry resides in the indissoluble unity of these two aspects.

(Ibid., p. 90)

The connection of both aspects should indeed be understood as indissoluble, but not merely because they need to be in a harmony, as common-sense opinion would have it.

As we have seen above, Dilthey denies the existence of any solid mental atoms, of any absolutely immutable pictures in the mind. If they existed, the function of our imagination would consist merely in recombining these immutable particles. On the contrary, the structure of the acquired psychic continuum regulates the perceived images in a more intrinsic and profound way. This is where we come to Dilthey's central doctrine of a 'metamorphosis of images' and 'formative processes'. Dilthey designates as a formative process any act of psychic structure, which makes an image change. According to Dilthey, such processes exist also on the level of cognitive and conative acts, but the formative power is most obvious in the sphere of feelings and affections.

The imagination as a spontaneous faculty accomplishes more than a perfect reproduction of something past. Dilthey distinguishes three main acts, by which memory images are transformed by feelings.[4] The first is *exclusion*, when some constituents of images 'either disappear or are excluded' (ibid., p. 102). Second, the *intensification* of an image means that 'the intensity of the sensations of which they are composed is increased or decreased' (ibid.). Both exclusion and intensification schematise and idealise the images in implicit accordance with our attention and interest. This is a simple way in which the psychic structure forms and controls the psychic contents. The third metamorphosing process, *completion*, is more complicated and is found more specifically in poetry. By completion, new components and connections penetrate into the innermost core of an image and complete it. The core of an image corresponds to the centre of acquired psychic continuum and we know that its periphery forms what is focused. For this reason Dilthey asserts:

Only when the whole acquired psychic nexus becomes active can images be transformed on the basis of it: innumerable, immeasurable, almost imperceptible changes occur in their nucleus. And in this way, the completion of the particular originates from the fullness of psychic life. Thus we obtain from images and their connections what is essential about a state of affairs: what gives it its meaning in the nexus of reality.

(Ibid., p. 104)[5]

It now becomes clear how lived experience provides the foundation for works of art. If every perceived image is formed by the psychic structure, the fact that we experience ourselves is constitutive for aesthetic experience; more accurately, an image or a sensorially accessible object symbolises or materialises our acquired life nexus (partially, of course) and makes it possible for us to experience this nexus. We 'enliven' something on the outside, when we place an individual image or idea in the centre of our psychic continuum and the image thereby becomes 'completed' by some other parts of this structure and, in short, becomes meaningful as a part of our experience.

Or, we can try to express our psychic continuum as a whole (predominant feeling, current mood, an inkling) through some perceptible things and events, reveal it in some sensitive material (the words of a poem, or the elements of a picture or a sculpture), which is in this way completed, too.

It needs to be underlined once again that 'lived experience' does not draw an objective thing in the sphere of private subjectivity. On the contrary, 'lived experience' first makes the outer things understandable both for us and for others. For us, because the acquired psychic nexus connects the perceptual image with the continuum of our experience; for others, because the psychic structure involves pre-subjective feelings and supra-individual cultural systems (such as acquired languages) that make our experience truly common and communicable.

However, we must not confuse this common nature of lived experience with an abstract universality. The content of any work of art, which has its substance in lived experience, cannot be translated into universal ideas *without remainder*. The lived experience is neither individual nor universal, it is *symbolic*. The things that we experience on the basis of the processes of metamorphosis are, paradoxically, individual universals. In this sense, a symbol is something that does not need to be universally shared by others, but which has a potential to found some new aspect of community and communication (as works of art really do).

Aesthetic experience does not strive for the same kind of universality as science does, although this attitude should not completely exclude an analytical and rational attitude towards the experience. In human studies, the aim is not to explore universality, but to describe what is particular, typical.[6] Correspondingly, the unity of *style* (characteristic for one artist, school, age) represents a type of universality that allows ethical and aesthetic discussions.

There is no room for a detailed discussion of Dilthey's *Poetics*. It will suffice to note that his aim was to elaborate a scientific foundation for traditional poetics and that he wanted to achieve it by the elaboration of the notion of the metamorphosis of images. He believed that he succeeded in tracing some of the laws of imagination, which determine the functioning of the psychic life in a strictly causal way.[7] The central part of *Poetics* is devoted to the classification of types of feelings and their combinations, which are seen as primary conditions of the processes of imagination. At that time, Dilthey was dealing with the idea that the poetic lexical means and techniques, such as metaphors, tropes, figures, rhythm or verses are directly dependent on the psychic processes and are their causal results.

When Dilthey was later preparing the second edition of his *Poetics*, he revised this idea. His preparatory drafts for the second edition show that the entire section on types of feelings and their effects on processes of metamorphosis of images had to be rewritten in order to avoid a quasi-causal way of speaking about psychic structure and imagination.[8] Instead of a causal–successive view of psychic processes, Dilthey now started to prefer more synchronic, structural account of the genesis of meaning.

Lived experience recontextualised and some questions on formative experience

We will now point out some limits of Dilthey's concept and its inherent difficulties, so as also to demonstrate, we hope, the potentialities for present-day theoretical thinking about experience and learning.

At first sight, the above account of Dilthey's aesthetics may seem to be closely connected to the understanding of the art and artists that was typical for Western countries at the end of the nineteenth century. In this era, art and aesthetic experience were largely considered as a specific sphere clearly separated from normal civic life. Correspondingly, the artist was admired and deemed to be an outstanding person. However, Dilthey was aware of the historical nature of every understanding of art and his perspective was surprisingly close to our times and such contemporary phenomena as street art and pop culture. His inquiry into the formative processes that occur in every human being leads to a significantly wider field than that occupied by traditional aesthetics and poetics. As Dilthey explains, this wider basis is constituted by the

> formative processes in which the representational contents and their connections are determined and formed *by the feelings*, without producing an impulse either to adapt external reality to the will or the will to reality. This can occur only in two cases. The first involves a

temporary equilibrium of feelings, in which life takes a holiday, as it were. Such an affective state is amplified, intensified and formed by festive enjoyment, social life, games and art.

(Ibid., p. 76; italics by Dilthey)

As we can see, Dilthey considers art as only one representative of a whole class of such complex phenomena as festivities, social life and games. Consequently, Dilthey's attempt to found poetics on psychology led him to foresee some basic topics of modern cultural and social anthropology.[9]

The above-mentioned social nature of the formative processes constituting the lived experience allows us to eliminate one striking difficulty in Dilthey's description of these processes. He characterises them as 'the transformations of representations beyond the bounds of reality' (ibid., p. 93). This formulation shows that there is an ambiguity in the way that Dilthey thinks about reality. Is it really possible to understand reality as something that allows us to form images of itself that are in turn transformed by psychic processes? Is it not more accurate to say that reality conceived of in this manner is only an abstraction, because it rests merely on the representative capacity of perception and thinking without respect to 'the whole of human nature', including our emotional and conative capacities?

Moreover, does it make sense to speak about 'representations of reality', if these representations do not consist of any solid and unchangeable parts? Dilthey was not an idealist denying the existence of the outer world, but he contended with the puzzle of how we can think of the relation between human being and world other than as of a complex of simple causal relations connecting things in the world. According to all evidence, he did not see any incoherence between taking the 'lived experience' as a model of the constitution of meaning and the notion of reality existing prior to being formed and acquiring a meaning on the basis of processes of metamorphosis.

However, we may ask, does meaningfulness belong to 'reality' or not? Dilthey probably saw no other alternative to idealism than a latent naturalism, which led him to describe the genesis of meaning in a quasi-causal way. This is attested by Dilthey's suggestion from his *Poetics* that we ought to distinguish reality and lived experience 'beyond the bounds of it'. Dilthey's compromises with the naturalistic approach are understandable only as an attempt to take a distance from the romantic tradition of 'the aesthetic worldview' (ibid., p. 45) according to which 'poetry was acknowledged as an independent power for intuiting the world and life ... [and] raised to an organon for understanding the world, alongside science and religion' (ibid.).

Now, as we have seen above, the activity of formative processes has wider scope than art or poetry in the nineteenth century's understanding. If we take a game or a social festivity as the model of a situation in which the formative processes are obviously active and where meaning is generated – for instance, the famous Wittgensteinian concept of 'language games', (Wittgenstein, 1971) – we can reconsider the personal aspect of lived experience. My experience does not arise from a neutral background of a purely objective nature, but rather from a particular social and cultural milieu, which contains cognitive and normative components, including of course some representations of nature. These components enter the individual continuum of psychic life, which provides the incessant intertwining of the inner and the outer (this is true for any kind of living being already at the physiological level).

Consequently, human life encounters nature only as socio-culturally mediated, not as some unformed 'raw' data; it rather confirms or rearranges the cultural patterns, which became 'natural' for us. In other words, the imaginative processes, as we propose to consider them, do not elevate natural sensations to artistic images, but rather confirm or transform the images implicitly used by a certain community in social communication. By enacting and revising the cultural images, words and ways of speaking, habitual schemata or behavioural stereotypes, each person realises 'the whole human nature'. And since this process of confirming or transforming cultural images involves conative and emotive moments, it is possible to say that it is always ethically relevant, because I must take an attitude towards them. Experiences which I must undergo and express by means of my imagination contribute, even if minimally, to the life of culture and its institutions. Not only artists are exceptional, but *everyone* participates in the 'poetics' of his or her culture. A meaning only arises as taken over through our understanding and our (social) acts.

Having briefly outlined how the problems inherent to Dilthey's *Poetics* could be resolved, we can now turn to the problem of the body and its role in Dilthey's concept of lived experience. Dilthey has clearly seen that our capacity to discern between the outer and the inner is dependent on the fact that our human existence evolves in a body and as a body. The body constitutes a boundary *sui generis*, because it can be observed as one thing among others (such as when I say that 'I *have* my body'), while on the other hand it is also on the side of the experiencing (such as when I say that 'I *am* my body'). Thus when for example a material obstacle restricts my conative act, I say that 'it restricts me', not that 'it restricts my body'. Embodied emotions, such as when I am moved in my heart, are also felt as taking place in 'me' rather than in 'my body'. In conative and emotive acts, my body usually belongs to 'me' – its place is on my side of the boundary. In contrast to that, representative acts have the capacity to present my body as an outer physical object among other objects (cf. Dilthey, 1989, p. 269).

In order properly to reconsider Dilthey's concept of lived experience, we must take into consideration that the processes of metamorphosis of images are based on the embodied nature of human beings. As Dilthey (1985, p. 105) explains, 'the way in which state and image are interwoven as inner and outer is not acquired, but rather is rooted in the psycho-physical nature of man'. If we take the freedom to go beyond Dilthey's verbatim formulations, we need to say that our body is *at once* an inner state and an outer image. Every act of perception is rooted in the feeling body and every movement and gesture is the expression of an image.

However, if we claim that feelings transform a 'perception' into an 'image beyond the bound of reality' and an act is their 'expression', it does not mean that there was an inner spiritual substance or idea that would come into appearance through the body. The expressive character of body must rather be thought of as continually referring to the acquired experience as a whole, which can only be *felt*. Inasmuch as it is meaningful, every living being's behaviour is built on this acquired experience.

Embodied living being must, of course, adopt an attitude in regard to its natural and social environment, but the most important feature of embodiment is that the living being's actions are not guided by natural and social 'objects' or impulses, but by the representations (images) it has of them. The dual faculty to perceive something as an image and to form images is united in the exceptional nature of feeling, which 'enlivens the images' and express itself in new images (in the body and through the body). The common ground for perception and moving (expression) resides in feeling, and the relation between the former two constitutes the cyclic structure of life.[10]

If we now remember our interpretation of reality as essentially social, we gain a new insight into the matter of what lived experience is. Our life is a social life because we have a body that feels. At first sight, this statement sounds rather paradoxical, because the body seems to isolate every living being in itself. However, our capacity to produce and receive images, which rests on our embodiment, presupposes a background where these images obtain their meaning. Above, we have described it as an acquired nexus, a continuum of experience. Now it is clear that human beings acquire experience often or even most of the time from experiences that they did not make personally. Nonetheless, other people's experience can become *my* experience – I am able to take them over. And, vice versa, my personal first-hand experience is shared by others. This socialising process is possible only as a process of translation of the sphere of the outer into the sphere of the inner (perception of images) and inversely (production of images).[11] As we have seen, this process is based on the imaginative power of embodiment, which possesses social, cultural and ethical dimension.

It is natural to ask whether such a general account of experience can serve to support some concrete aim. It is clear at least that such a general philosophical account has the potential to inspire us to think about formative experiences in a more open-minded way. According to Dilthey, there are no firm frontiers between ethical, aesthetical and cognitive spheres, although it makes good sense to discern them. He shows that humans form their experience as social and embodied beings, as subjects who must communicate with their environment and differentiate themselves from it. Dilthey's central thought, according to which every particular human experience expresses 'the whole human nature', certainly has strong relevance for anybody whose task is to evaluate or even shape human experience, such as an educator.

For this idea invites us to take into account that even a physical movement, for instance, is realised by a social being, or that as an embodied being, the human subject is also a moral one. In other words, formative experiences are not defined by a particular activity or procedure; their formative potential consists in the extent to which one particular event is able to embrace (and so to transform) the many-sided human nature. From a more philosophical point of view, Dilthey's research on different types and spheres of feelings provides a model of how something as general as experience, and human existence in its world, can be studied and described in a quite concrete way.[12]

Notes

1 Subsequently referred to only as *Poetics*. All quotations are from the English translation by L. Agosta and R. L. Makkreel, Dilthey (1985, pp. 29–173).

2 Regarding Dilthey's role in the subsequent development of twentieth century's philosophical anthropology, see Lessing (2016b, pp. 99–110).

3 The compound phrase 'lived experience' used by the translators of *Selected Works* aims to reproduce the semantic segment *-leb-* included in the German noun *Erlebnis* (*leben* means 'to live'). The noun *Erlebnis* itself is a derivative from the verb *erleben* 'to make (lived) experience'. The noun first appears in German around 1815, the verb in the second half of eighteenth century. These two expressions (*Erlebnis, erleben*) came into vogue in the period of romanticism and sentimentalism and unlike the common German word for experience (*Erfahrung*), they accentuate the personal and subjective aspects of experience. For a more detailed analysis see Sauerland (1972, pp. 1–27).

4 For Dilthey, the boundary between perception and memory was more sharp and solid than for subsequent generations of thinkers. In particular Husserl's

phenomenological analysis of time (Husserl, 1966) has elucidated that the act of perception is constituted also by the retention (immediate recollection) and protention (anticipation). In other words, even perception itself necessarily contains some imaginative components. Taking up this discovery will allow us to radicalise Dilthey's philosophical project.

5 It ought to be noted, however, that the formulation is misleading insofar as the whole acquired psychic structure is, to some extent, active in every psychic act; cf. Makkreel (1991, pp. 130–149) and Rodi (2003, pp. 85–106). It might be argued against Dilthey's account of 'formative processes' that the things of our common experience usually display quite stable features. But the usual stability of our experience, Dilthey would say, is also a result of processes of psychic structure. The formative processes are mostly directed by our practical interests and so the images are schematised (by acts of exclusion and intensification) according to tasks of our will (and under stabilising influence of social habits and language).

6 Cf. Makkreel (1968).

7 In fact, Dilthey was influenced by the physiologist J. Müller, who believed that he had discovered the sensorial–physiological roots of imagination. Another naturalistic inspiration for Dilthey was the experimental psychologist G. Fechner and his aesthetics based on describing psychological causal laws. For a description of Dilthey's early concept of imagination and its relation to Müller's reformulation of Goethe's idea of metamorphosis see Rodi (2003, pp. 85–106) and Lessing (2016a, pp. 98–113).

8 See Dilthey (1958, pp. 307–320). *Selected Works* only contain fragments that are among the more coherent (Dilthey, 1985, pp. 223–231). Cf. also Müller-Vollmer (1963, pp. 187–196). Dilthey's 1906/1907 plans for rewriting the *Poetics* have remained unaccomplished. However, the revised version of his famous essay *Goethe and the Poetic Imagination* from 1910 shows clearly which modifications Dilthey intended. The concept of psychic structure did not lose its prominence but was connected with the category of meaning (*Bedeutung*), whereas the doctrine about three ways of metamorphosis of images was mentioned only marginally – see Dilthey (1985, p. 241).

9 Cf. the well-known definition of religious symbols by Clifford Geertz. According to him, their meaningfulness consists in the connection of normative and descriptive aspects. The religious symbols (for example the yin-yang or the Cross) show *at once* what the world looks like and how we have to behave in it. The connection or intertwining of the both aspects suggests that the world is not an absurd place for our existence and that we rather fit into it; see Geertz (1973, pp. 126–141).

10 From this point of view, Dilthey appears as a pioneer of Gestalt psychology and some currents in recent biology (biosemiotics). See Rodi (2016, pp. 51–69), de Mul (2013).

11 The deliberated emphasis on the communicative aspect of art represents a truly innovative feature of Dilthey's Aesthetic. His concept of lived experience can serve as a foundation to reconcile two traditionally opposed approaches: the inquiries into the reception of aesthetic objects, aesthetic pleasure, and taste on the one hand, and the analysis of artistic creativity on the other.

12 Some currents of recent philosophy are really going this way. Cf. for example Colombetti (2014).

Bibliography

Colombetti, G. (2014). *The Feeling Body. Affective Science Meets the Enactive Mind.* Cambridge. MA: The MIT Press.

de Mul, J. (2013). *Understanding Nature. Dilthey, Plessner and Biohermeneutics.* In: D'Anna, G., Johach, H. and Nelson, E. J., eds, *Anthopologie und Geschichte. Studien zu Wilhelm Dilthey aus Anlass seines 100. Todestages.* Würzburg: Königshausen & Neumann, pp. 459–478.

Dilthey, W. (1958). *Die geistige Welt, II. Abhandlungen zur Poetik, Ethik und Pädagogik. Gesammelte Schriften, VI.* Stuttgart – Göttingen: Teubner – Vandenhoeck & Ruprecht.

Dilthey, W. (1985). *Poetry and Experience. Selected Works,* eds R. A. Makkreel and F. Rodi, Vol. V. Princeton: Princeton University Press.

Dilthey, W. (1989). *Introduction to the Human Sciences. Selected Works,* eds R. A. Makkreel and F. Rodi, Vol. I. Princeton: Princeton University Press.

Dilthey, W. (1997). *Psychologie als Erfahrungwissenschaft I., Vorlesungen zur Psychologie und Anthropologie (c.*1875–1894), eds G. Kerekhoven and H. U. Lessing. Göttingen: Vandenhoeck & Ruprecht.

Geertz, C. (1973). *The Interpretation of Cultures. Selected Essays.* New York: Basic Books

Herrmann, U. (1971). *Die Pädagogik Wilhelm Diltheys. Ihr wissenschaftstheoretischer Ansatz in Diltheys' Theorie der Geisteswissenschaften.* Göttingen: Vandenhoeck & Ruprecht.

Husserl, E. (1966). *Zur Phänomenologie des inneren Zeitbewusstseins (1893–1917),* ed. R. Boehm (Husserliana, X). Haag: Martinus Nijhoff.

Lessing, H.-U. (2016a). *Die Autonomie der Geisteswissenschaften. Studien zur Philosophie Wilhelm Diltheys.* Bd. I. *Dilthey im philosophie- und wissenschaftsgeschichtlichen Kontext.* Bautz: Traugott.

Lessing, H.-U. (2016b). *Die Autonomie der Geisteswissenschaften. Studien zur Philosophie Wilhelm Diltheys.* Bd. II. *Systematische Untersuchungen zu Diltheys Werk.* Bautz: Traugott.

Makkreel, R. A. (1968). Toward a Concept of Style: An Interpretation of Wilhelm Dilthey's Psycho-Historical Account of the Imagination. *Journal of Aesthetics and Art Criticism* 27/2.

Makkreel, R. A. (1991). *Dilthey. Philosoph der Geisteswissenschaften.* Frankfurt am Main: Suhrkamp.

Müller-Vollmer, K. (1963). *Towards a Phenomenological Theory of Literature. A Study of Wilhelm Dilthey's Poetik.* The Hague: Mouton & Co.

Rodi, F. (2003). *Das strukturierte Ganze. Studien zum Werk von Wilhelm Dilthey.* Weilerswist: Velbrück Wissenschaft.

Rodi, F. (2016). *Diltheys Philosophie des Lebenszusammenhangs. Strukturtheorie – Hermeneutik – Anthropologie.* Freiburg – München: Karl Alber Verlag.

Sauerland, K. (1972). *Diltheys Erlebnisbegriff. Entstehnug, Glanzzeit und Verkümmerung eines literaturhistorischen Begriffs.* Berlin – New York: Walter de Gruyter.

Wittgenstein, L. (1971). *Philosophische Untersuchungen.* Frankfurt am Main: Suhrkamp.

5 Learning as differentiation of experiential schemas

Jan Halák

Introduction

The goal of this chapter is to provide an interpretation of experiential learning that fully detaches itself from the epistemological presuppositions of empiricist and intellectualist accounts of learning. I first introduce the concept of schema as understood by Kant and I explain how it is related to the problems implied by the empiricist and intellectualist frameworks. I then interpret David Kolb's theory of learning that is based on the concept of learning cycle and represents an attempt to overcome the corresponding drawbacks of these frameworks. I show that Kolb's theory fails to achieve its goal because it is rooted in some of the fundamental epistemological presuppositions of these frameworks. Subsequently, I present a group of works from phenomenology, in particular Merleau-Ponty's, in order to show that Kolb's attempt is insufficient due to a lack of understanding of the problem expressed by Kant via the concept of schema. Finally, I outline an interpretation of experiential learning as differentiation of experiential schemas and explain how it meets the epistemological challenges outlined above.

Kant's idea of schematism

A comprehensive theory of learning from experience must tackle an ancient epistemological, that is, philosophical problem: how an experience that is relatively limited in time and space leads to a knowledge that becomes, ideally, independent of the particular situation from which it stems, and thereby acquires a general value.

Correspondingly, one of the first answers to the question of learning from experience is given by one of the founders of Western philosophical tradition, Plato. His suggestion, however, is less a solution of the above problem then its refusal. In his view, we never really learn *from* the experience. To learn, Plato claims, is rather to 'recollect' what is intelligible and what exists independently of experience and is accessed *before* it is inserted into a sensible, bodily, historical situation (see *Meno*, Cooper and Hutchinson, 1997, pp. 880–886; *Phaedo*, ibid., pp. 63–67). For Plato then, the world that we experience cannot be the source of knowledge, because its reality is only an imitation of the original realities, the intelligible 'ideas'. From this point of view, learning consists of removing the obstruction that eclipses the true reality by means of proper inquiry. The concrete situation *from which* learning has to begin does not play any positive role here and there is therefore no room for a true experiential learning.

A position that is completely opposed to Plato's, but similarly refusing the problem, is defended for instance by the behaviourist school. From its radically empiricist perspective, the only source of knowledge is the external environmental pressure to which a subject is exposed. Such an epistemological position, however, misrepresents one the fundamental aspects of knowledge, the generality. The plurality of empirical processes or events that sum up only produce an *appearance of* generality: what we learn cannot be understood as more knowledge about one phenomenon, but merely a different sum of elements.

The learning theories based on aprioristic and empiricist epistemologies are both one-sided and have the obvious drawback that they call for each other. A theory of learning must respect that we *transcend* our situation *on the basis of* that situation, that we acquire more knowledge about something but also that we initially truly ignore some of its aspects.

A more complex answer to the problem of linkage between what we learn about and what we learn it on is offered by Kant. He believes that there is not one, but two 'sources' that correspond to concrete and general aspects of experience: receptive sensibility and spontaneous understanding. Making a strict distinction between, on the one hand, sensible intuitions, and pure concepts and forms of intuition on the other, Kant's epistemology is *hylemorphic*. In order to have an actual experience, the two sources of experience must each contribute to it: an intuitively graspable sensorial matter (*hyle*) must be organised or shaped by intelligible rules or forms (*morphe*).

The problem faced by Kant is then to explain how the general forms of understanding or 'categories', which are heterogeneous from the concrete sensible appearances (see Kant, 1999, p. 271), can be applied to them, that is, how they can be united with a qualitative, but as-yet unorganised sensorial experiential matter. Now it is quite clear, Kant points out, that 'there must be *a third thing*, which must stand in homogeneity with the category on the one hand and the appearance on the other, and makes possible the application of the former to the latter' (ibid., p. 272; emphasis mine). The third thing that provides a solution to that problem is called by Kant the 'transcendental schematism' (see Kant, 1999, pp. 271–277).

In short, Kant's transcendental schemas are supplementary rules or procedures for interpreting conceptual rules in terms of more specific figural (spatiotemporal) forms and sensory images (see, e.g. Hanna, 2018; Matherne, 2016). Kant discusses several types of schematism according to their position on the scale between the concrete and the general. As an example of 'pure sensible' schematism Kant discusses mathematical concepts. They too have the particular characteristics of presenting a purely formal content through experientially accessible phenomena: the meaning of mathematical concepts is radically independent of the actual development of experience (which is why Kant calls them 'pure'), but they are also observable in concrete, perceptually given situations.[1] The idea of 1,000, for instance, is accessible to the intelligence as a pure form of quantity, unlike a group of 1,000 dots drawn on a paper: the latter cannot be grasped as being precisely 1,000, while the former cannot be experienced anywhere in the perceptible world. The *number* of 1,000, however, is a schema of the category of quantity, which means that it secures the procedure of linking the group of 1,000 empirical elements to the idea of 1,000, thereby securing the evidence that these elements in fact instantiate the absolutely non-empirical idea of quantity. In sum, a Kantian schema makes it possible for us to link a concrete experience of a perceptually accessible situation with a general, non-empirical idea, and vice versa. This is only possible because the schema precisely *organises* the way in which the two aspects of experience, which are understood as distinct and separate in the hylemorphic framework, relate to each other.

Since schemas are linked to 'sensory images', Kant believes that they are produced by imagination, unlike all the intellectual contents that do not involve any sensorial aspects. However, Kant's description of the role of imagination in experience, and by its proxy of schematism, is ambiguous. If schematism is required as a factor mediating between the sensibility and understanding, the imagination producing the schematism should be understood as a *third* original source of experience, as some of Kant's own formulations suggest. Yet on different occasions, Kant subordinates imagination, and by its proxy the schematism, to the sensibility, or to the understanding. By doing that, he reaffirms his initial hylemorphic epistemological framework and, in fact, dismisses the idea of schema as an original aspect of experience. And Kant proceeds in this way for a good reason, for if he fully embraced the idea of schema as an original source of experience, he might need to abandon his hylemorphic framework and thus the ideas of pure forms and matter of experience. Our experience would then only involve schemas, various instances of *formed matter*.[2] This would, in turn, require us to completely recast the interpretation of both intellectual and sensory experience because they would turn out to be two types of experience based on schemas. For this reason, the concept of schema might be compared with the idea of *Gestalt* (figure) as introduced by Gestalt psychology.[3]

Kant's primary concern is epistemological, but as we saw in the beginning, the epistemological difficulty Kant attempts to resolve by introducing the concept of schematism has fundamental importance for the problem of learning. By asking how a concrete given situation can be integrated into the framework of general knowledge and thus eventually transform it, or inversely, how a conceptual framework can shed light on a concrete situation and make us understand it better, we are already inquiring into the problem of learning.

The question is then whether there is a learning theory that would satisfactorily answer the problem of learning in a similar way that the Kantian idea of schematism answers to the problem of experience. Based on this perspective, the following two sections of this chapter will attempt to discuss two attempts to overcome the one-sidedness of the empiricist–objectivistic and intellectualist–subjectivistic theories of learning: Kolb's 'learning cycle' and Merleau-Ponty's account of experience based on the idea of experiential norms that have the function of schemas.

Kolb's learning cycle

By asserting that 'to understand learning, we must understand epistemology', David Kolb defines the problem of learning in very similar terms to those I used at the beginning of this chapter (Kolb, 2015, p. 48). His 'experiential learning theory' (2015, first published 1984) is an example of a relatively sophisticated conceptual framework that attempts to integrate the thoughts of a number of authors usually associated with learning from experience. Kolb discusses the positions of Dewey, James, Lewin, Piaget and other philosophers, psychologists, sociologists and educational theorists. He attempts to synthesise their thoughts under the heading of the concept of a 'learning cycle' or 'spiral' (see in particular Kolb, 2015, p. 51, figure 2.5; ibid., p. 186). Correspondingly, the process of experiential learning is described by Kolb as 'a four-stage cycle involving four adaptive learning modes – concrete experience, reflective observation, abstract conceptualisation, and active experimentation' (ibid., p. 66). I will now analyse Kolb's theory from an epistemological point of view in order to see whether it meets the challenge to provide an epistemological basis for a comprehensive theory of learning from experience.

The four 'modes' that are supposed to govern our relation to the world, and therefore play a key role in learning, are defined by Kolb as mutually 'opposed' (ibid., p. 66), 'distinct' (ibid.) and 'independent' from each other (ibid., p. 8). Importantly, Kolb also strongly emphasises that we must understand these modes as 'coequal' (e.g. ibid., p. 76). That is, none of them is subordinated to any other, unlike in the theories that I have discussed earlier on the examples of Plato and behaviourism. In reference to the above discussion of Kant, it can be said that Kolb's experiential modes are four 'sources' of experience that are distinct, yet all original and mutually irreducible.

Kolb more precisely groups the four experiential modes into two couples related respectively to our 'prehension' or the 'processes of grasping or taking hold of experience in the world', and to our 'transformation' of the world (ibid., p. 67). The two opposed modes of *prehension* are based either on reliance 'on the tangible, felt qualities of immediate experience' (apprehension), or on 'conceptual interpretation and symbolic representation' (comprehension) (ibid.). In turn, the two opposed modes of *transformation* of our environment are based either on 'internal reflection' or 'external manipulation' (ibid.).

As evident from Kolb's definitions, the four modes of experiencing correspond to some of the traditional Western conceptual dichotomies: the apprehension is linked to the ideas of immediate, felt, qualitative contents given in individual experience, as opposed to comprehension, which is intellectual, intersubjectively shared, formal, linked to the use of symbols, and therefore culturally and inter-personally mediated. The manipulation and reflection are respectively associated with the subject's exterior and interior, and to action and passive receptivity. Moreover, the apprehension is identified with '*subjective* personal process that cannot be known by others' except via communication based on comprehension; and inversely, comprehension with 'an *objective* social process' (ibid., p. 159; emphasis mine).

The idea of learning as a movement through stages of a cycle implies that the opposite modes of experience lead to learning when they are put into relation through a 'successive iteration' (ibid., p. 186). As Kolb puts it, the experience in general, and learning from experience in particular, are produced on the basis of an 'interaction', 'transaction', 'interrelation' or 'dialectics' between the four opposed experiential modes. I will now analyse this idea in more detail.

As I have already noted, Kolb strongly emphasises that the modes are distinct and opposed. This fact contrasts with the weakness of his explanation of the supposed interrelation between these opposites. In fact, Kolb does not even offer his own account, but refers to Kant's claim that experience is produced through combining understanding and sensibility:

The essence of the interrelationship is expressed in Kant's analysis of their interdependence: Apprehensions are the source of validation for comprehensions ('thoughts without content are empty'), and comprehensions are the source of guidance in the selection of apprehensions ('intuitions without concepts are blind').

(Ibid., p. 160; alluding to Kant, 1999, pp. 193–194)

In other words, the apprehension should 'validate' abstract structures of knowledge through a 'contact with the world in … immediate perception'; and inversely, 'comprehension is capable of selecting and reshaping apprehended experience' (Kolb, 2015, p. 160). In Kolb's view thus, the role of apprehension is to provide 'contents' of experience, whereas the role of apprehension is to 'select' and 'shape' those contents (as opposed to merely representing the contents; cf. ibid.). It ought to be noted right away, however, that Kolb's claim of an 'interdependence' between apprehension and comprehension (see ibid., pp. 160–161), contradicts his earlier claims according to which all four modes are 'distinct' (ibid., p. 66) and 'independent' (ibid., p. 81). Moreover, if we accept that apprehension and comprehension are originally interdependent, we cannot define learning as a transaction between these two dimensions, for this would mean to abolish the difference between learning and experience in general.

In order to clarify the relations and the process of dynamic exchanges between the experiential modes, Kolb also speaks of 'dialectics'. Although the concept of dialectics seems to be crucial for him, his explanation of that concept is, similarly to his account of 'interrelation', surprisingly weak. It is only later in his book that Kolb starts alluding to the 'Hegelian' dialectics (ibid., p. 155) and eventually applies a very general account of Hegel's idea to his own categories of apprehension and comprehension: the relation of these processes is supposed to be 'dialectical' because, although they 'cannot be entirely explained in terms of the other', they supposedly 'merge towards a higher truth that encompasses and transcends them' (ibid., p. 162). Unfortunately, this formulation does not provide any insight into how the merging is concretely operated by the learner. The claim that there is *de facto* merging of what has been defined as *de jure* distinct and independent is unconvincing and does not bring any better understanding. The concept of dialectics is thus no less clear than the metaphors of circle and transaction.

Significantly, Kolb's perhaps most direct attempt to describe the relation between apprehension and comprehension is not at all relevant for epistemological discussion of learning. Kolb in fact suggests the adoption of 'an attitude of partial scepticism in which the knowledge of comprehension is held provisionally to be tested against apprehensions, and vice versa' (ibid., p. 163). This is a psychological description that might have some practical relevance, but it does not advance our understanding of learning as an epistemological problem: the scepticism and dogmatism (mentioned earlier in Kolb's text) are themselves epistemological positions that are originally defined one in opposition to another. Kolb posits these opposites as simultaneously valid, but his suggestion to practically combine them is impossible to follow, for we still do not know *where exactly to put the limits* to scepticism and dogmatism which are two positions excluding each other. As Kolb eventually notes himself, it is thus 'somewhat mysterious' how precisely the 'dialectical synthesis' of the four distinct experiential modes is achieved (ibid., p. 162).

In sum, a closer look on the epistemological grounds of Kolb's account of learning shows that the conceptual framework it relies on is burdened with contradictions and does not clarify how the elements of experience, which have been initially dissociated, should, and ever could, be linked back together. The interdependence of experiential modes is taken as a fact, although this contradicts how the conceptual framework is designed. While there is no doubt that humans, in fact, review or reassess their 'concrete' experiences in the light of 'general' (sometimes conceptual) frameworks and vice versa, Kolb's account of experience does not help us to understand why and how this is possible. One may agree with Kolb's claim that discussions based on the idea of an 'idealized learning cycle' may have some 'pragmatic utility' (ibid., p. 57) or serve as *a particular type of* instructional guideline in practical situations. It is however not clear how they could serve as an epistemologically sound framework for a *general* theory of learning from experience.

Kolb's attempt implies that we either explain how learning is produced from an interaction between strictly distinct modes of experience, or we must abandon the idea that they are distinct. Although he advocates the former position, Kolb in fact does not provide any explanation in which the distinctness of the modes would be taken seriously. If learning consisted in a 'transaction' between the 'concrete' and the 'general' on the one hand, and between an 'action' and 'reflection' on the other, we would be imprisoned in symmetrical operations of generalisation and application (induction and deduction), pure activity and pure observation, without any possibility for learning. If we conceive the concrete as *nothing but* concrete, it does not have any general validity; and since it cannot be linked to anything general, the concrete and the general cannot transform each other and lead to learning. As we have seen earlier, this problem leads Kant to introduce the concept of schema: if one wants to posit distinct experiential modes, one has to provide a *supplementary* factor regulating the way in which the two heterogeneous dimensions relate to each other.[4] Similarly, if action is conceived as pure action which does not involve any observation, it is not clear how it can ever be informed by it. In general, therefore, if the moments of the 'learning cycle' are defined and truly understood as mutually exclusive, general ideas must be magically applied to absolutely new concrete cases, or inversely, deduced from them; and similarly, the action must magically spurt from nowhere, without motivation, while the observation must be zero of action. The gap between these mutually exclusive extremes is not filled by verbally announcing that there is a 'transaction' or 'dialectics' between them. Without a conceptual element similar to Kant's schematism of experience, Kolb's theory is paralysed.

It is also worth noting that a number of Kolb's own remarks and more particular discussions relativise his epistemological framework based on a rather uncritical combination of empiricist (apprehension, external action) and intellectualist claims (comprehension, internal reflexion). Kolb states, for instance, that 'thinking and reflection can continue for some time before acting and experiencing' (ibid., p. 57). If this is true (as it does seem to be), how are we to differentiate between action and reflection and manage the shift from one attitude to another which is required for learning? Similarly, if social knowledge 'cannot exist independently of the knower', as Kolb claims (ibid., p. 159), the comprehension and apprehension cannot first be defined as distinct and independent from each other. Moreover, if knowledge 'requires active learners to interact with, interpret, and elaborate' the symbols and symbolic systems in which it is deposited (ibid., p. 174), reflection cannot first be defined in opposition to action. In all these and many similar cases, Kolb's theoretical framework is not up to par with his concrete observations and, as it seems, his actual intentions. (As I explained, although he posits the modes as distinct, Kolb is himself interested principally in their *interaction*. Similarly, Kolb's inventory of learning styles (see ibid., pp. 97–151) seems to be based more on a *ratio* between the modes, not really on their distinctness and opposition.)

With the relativisation of the conceptual oppositions that stand at the basis of Kolb's theoretical framework, we come to the idea that the modes of experience he evokes do not correspond to any real elements or experience, because *all* experiences contain *all* of those modes. This observation has then fundamental implications for our definition of learning, because the latter can no longer be defined as a transaction *between* the experiential modes.

Merleau-Ponty on perceptual norms

Kolb asserts that our experience involves 'concrete', 'felt', 'immediate' experiences (2015, p. 67), 'a seamless, unpredictable flow of apprehended sensations' (ibid., p. 69).[5] Assuming that he identified one of the modes of the 'learning cycle', he then assigns this presumed element of experience an important role in learning: when an immediate apprehension such as perception *disrupts* one's ordinary, 'habitual' experience, we make a step in the learning cycle, that is, we learn (see ibid., p. 59). However, there are good reasons to believe that to oppose perceptual experience and the habitual experience, as well as all other Kolb's experiential 'modes', is to misrepresent perception and experience in general. In order to clarify this problem, I will now examine in detail the relation between perception and the original habituality of embodied behaviour as described by Merleau-Ponty. I will then confront this phenomenological account with Kolb's theory of learning based on the distinct character of four experiential modes.

In *Phenomenology of Perception*, Merleau-Ponty showed that we need to understand our body as the 'primordial habit' because it provides the necessary guidance in our encounters with perceived environment (Merleau-Ponty, 2012, p. 93).[6] I can only perceive inasmuch as my body mobilises some of its powers that are already available to me as a 'habitual knowledge' (ibid., p. 247), an original acquisition of typical ways in which it proceeds. A sensation calls for some corporeal capacities upon which I do not decide. I see colours because my body is sensitive to them and I just 'lend' it to the spectacle: I adjust my posture, I direct my gaze towards an object and follow its contours without questioning my body's 'system of anonymous "functions"', its 'perceptual tradition' (ibid., pp. 265, 247–248). Perception, claims Merleau-Ponty, 'is not a personal act' but rather a 'prepersonal' or 'impersonal' one (ibid., pp. 224, 249; cf. Hainämaa, 2015).

The fact that the subject of perception is a 'general existence' corresponding to our 'incarnate and habitual being' (ibid. p., 224; Merleau-Ponty, 1970, p. 6) is connected to other important implications. First of all, as a general capacity to relate to the world, my body possess an originally *inter*-personal value. Precisely because the structures of my body are something that I share with all other humans, and even with animals to some extent, I experience other living beings as others *of my kind* (see, e.g. Husserl on 'empathy', 2013, §§42–62). Correspondingly, corporeal behavioural patterns on which perception relies, such as upright posture, and more in general all corporeal skills that are ontogenetically acquired, are inter-corporeally formed as well as transferrable. Contrary to what Kolb claims thus, perception cannot be interpreted as the 'personal knowledge of individuals' and straightforwardly opposed to 'social knowledge' (Kolb, 2015, pp. 187, 186).

Moreover, even the most elementary corporeal experience such as a perceptual sensation presupposes subject's 'prospective activity' realised by means of factual corporeal movements (Merleau-Ponty, 2012, p. 241). A sensorial 'quality', explains Merleau-Ponty, is experienced originally as 'a certain mode of movement or of behaviour' (ibid., p. 243).[7] The sensible is given to me as a solicitation for my bodily powers and 'I must find the attitude that *will* provide it with the means to become determinate' and given to its fullest (ibid., p. 222; original emphasis). I need to 'subtend' the colour with an appropriate stance and exploratory movements as I need to follow the form of an object with my hand if I want to touch it. Since the so-called 'sensible qualities', such as colours, are originally 'presented with a motor physiognomy' (ibid., p. 217) and 'intend' a particular type of grasping (ibid., p. 219), they are not reducible to directly apprehended facts that would subsist independently of all context. The perceptual and motor aspect of perception 'communicate' with each other (ibid., p. 217), and Merleau-Ponty claims even more radically that they are 'synonymous' (Merleau-Ponty, 1968, p. 255). There is no observation without active involvement, and inversely, no action is blind. We must look in order to see something, and inversely, to look is to open a field of something to be seen.

More precisely, the sensation of red for example, does not *cause* 'red motor behaviour', that is, a movement of abduction. The sensation can be produced, or inversely eclipsed, only by the colour context (cf. Merleau-Ponty, 2012, p. 217). A particular motor behaviour is therefore not produced simply by the physical phenomenon of light of a particular wavelength externally affecting a particular segment of the body as a physical object. Rather, perception is holistic: a perceived colour represents a particular *situation* into which my body is inserted, and which requires a typical act of adaptation on my part. The situation involves potentially very different physicochemical elements each time and my response to it can be composed of different elements, such as when I replace the action of one limb by another. The subject thus reacts not by associating a particular action to particular objective stimulus, but rather by responding 'with a certain type of solution to a certain form of situation' (ibid., p. 143).

What is more, sensations are correlated to bodily attitudes and motor behaviours in a precognitive way. Such as in the case of very weak or brief stimuli, the subject does not need to 'feel' a sensation of red or be explicitly aware of it in order to engage in a 'red behaviour'. Before eventually acquiring an explicit cognitive value, all sensorial qualities have 'vital significance', because they are modulations of 'a certain general arrangement by which I am adapted to the world' (ibid., pp. 219, 218). Since red and yellow, for example, induce a movement of abduction, they accordingly accentuate errors in the estimation of weight and of time (ibid., p. 217). Sensations, such as colours, thus have normative behavioural value even prior to being consciously and intellectually assessed.

To perceive therefore *does not mean* to relate two distinct and opposed dimensions, to 'validate and test abstract concepts' in the light of 'here-and-now concrete experience' (Kolb, 2015, p. 32). A perceived object as such is a 'total configuration', or a schema, distributing and organising different perceptual values so as to originally appear as various aspects of a single object given in various circumstances (cf. Merleau-Ponty, 2012, p. 251).[8] Only because all the shades of a piece of paper are organised into one *Gestalt* in an original way, I experience them originally as phenomena of a white piece of paper, without ever encountering them as disparate sensations of 'grey', 'yellow', etc. and needing to intellectually synthesise the latter into an abstract idea of the object (cf. ibid., pp. 318–327).

Merleau-Ponty furthermore explains that our experience is originally schematised, that is, organised into meaningful wholes, because it correlates with the original organic unity of the body (see, e.g. ibid., p. 241). Not incidentally, Merleau-Ponty describes the unity of the body with help from the notion of the 'body schema', which he adopts from neurology and opposes both to sensorial 'image' of the body and its intellectual representation (cf. in particular ibid., pp. 239–244, 2011, pp. 126–165; for a more recent account, see Gallagher, 2005). The mutual organisation of bodily parts, which determines the range of actions on the basis of which the body relates to its environment, is reflected in the organisation of the perceived objects. This fact is clearly visible in situations forcing the subject to reorganise his/her body schema and thus accommodate his/her perceptual 'norms'. Merleau-Ponty's interpretation of some corporeal pathologies or experiments related to our perception of spatial orientation and depth suggest that a particular perception is not dependent merely on a subject's attitude and the structure of the spectacle, but more complexly on how the subject anchors his actions in the environment and how the latter supports the former, be it only virtually. Similarly, a particular colour of an object only appears as 'determined in relation to a [perceptual] level that is variable' according to how our body actively interacts with the environment (Merleau-Ponty, 2012, p. 324).

In sum, even the most elementary perceptual experiences are not of individual cases, but of situations. As such, they have an original systematic value and serve as reference norms for other experiences. In other words, perceived objects '*direct* our gaze rather than arresting it' (ibid., p. 323; original emphasis). As footholds for the movement of my exploration and linkage of perceptual elements, the perceptual norms are themselves established in relation to the capacities of my body to explore, and vary correspondingly as to how these capacities evolve or deteriorate.

Experiential norms and learning

Merleau-Ponty's account of perception has by itself important implications for our understanding of learning. Some of these implications were outlined by Merleau-Ponty himself, some others by the commentators of his works, in particular in connection to his interpretation of corporeal habits.[9] Most importantly in our context, Merleau-Ponty's conceptual framework reveals an experiential structure that is identifiable beyond embodied experiences and which seems to be absent from all hylemorphic accounts. As Merleau-Ponty's examples discussed above suggest, the epistemological function of experiential 'norms' is to organise experiential contents at different points of time and space, but unlike Kant's *a priori* forms, they are also open to transformations depending on the structure of those contents. This is where learning comes into play. A closer look at this point should help us to clarify in what respect Merleau-Ponty's epistemology offers correction to Kolb's idea of learning cycle.

As both Talero (2006, p. 201) and Howell (2015, p. 327) point out drawing on Merleau-Ponty, one's capacity to experience new situations is not based on the fact that they would simply *contradict* one's habits, as in Kolb's view. On the contrary, it is precisely one's habitual existence and the pre-established experiential norms that originally open up possibilities of some situations to be encountered, including those in fact never experienced. As I walk down the street and turn into an alley that I have never been in before, my capacities to identify vertical orientation, keep myself upright and maintain balance as I continue to walk are perfectly sufficient even though this situation is factually 'new' to me. It is only when I attempt to walk on a tightrope, for example, that my past standards of orientation and maintaining an upright stance are challenged.

First of all, then, the account of perception based on the concept of norms reveals that the apparent immediacy of sensual apprehension, which is cherished by empiricist philosophers and referred to by many theorists of 'experiential' learning, is an effect that is produced only in certain limits. That is, only insomuch as the appearing phenomenon is precisely *compliant* with the pre-established norms of habitual actions and the fundamental mediating role of the norm is precluded (cf. Howell, 2015, p. 326). Empiricist philosophers developed their concept of sensation without taking into account precisely those situations in which the effect of immediacy is challenged, that is, in which the perceived situation necessitates a re-establishment of our referential norms and pushes us to a new type of stance, attitude, movement or behaviour. Paradoxically thus, learning theories referring to 'purely sensorial' experience, such as Kolb's one, are based on an account of sensory experience *from which all learning situations are methodically excluded.* It is then no surprise that they relegate learning to a relation with 'abstract' ideas.

By contrast, Merleau-Ponty's epistemology bring us to the idea that experiential learning has to be understood in relation to how a situation as a whole reorganises normative standards based on which we experience them in the first place, no matter how 'abstract' or 'concrete' the experience is. By consequence, it becomes clear that the distinction between concrete and abstract experience does not match the difference between the singularity of the situation (which is *where* we learn from) and the general meaning of the situation (which is *what* we learn). This difference must be identified as the difference between a global schema or norm and a more specifically organised, or differentiated, schema.

For instance, the situation of tightrope walking is a variant of the situation of upright standing and walking on the ground. If I improve my skill by gradually incorporating other more subtle elements of my motor capacities into the new situation, not only do I henceforth experience tightropes as walkable, but I also perceive *all* elements of my environment as potential references to the activity-type 'tightrope walking', as solicitations and footholds for it. My experiential schemas are reorganised and my norms of how to relate to elements of my environment are re-established, which is an event having nothing to do with generalisation. The process of learning bodily skills corresponds to more finely differentiating among the structures of situations rather than of learning to integrate discrete bits of sensory information into an abstract unity (cf. Howell, 2015, pp. 332–333; Marratto, 2012, p. 69).

Similarly, when children learn to differentiate between colours, they do not start to deductively subsume colours, given in the form of distinctly felt positive sensations or 'contents', under pre-existing general concepts of colours (deposited in language, for example). Neither do they, of course, just inductively construct the latter on the basis of the former. A neophyte's colour space is not initially filled with unconnected distinct sensations, but rather undifferentiated and only globally organised. The process through which neophytes start to differentiate colours then correlates with the development of their motor skills even before a proper understanding of language and 'abstract' thinking comes into play (Merleau-Ponty, 2012, p. 32; cf. Marratto, 2012, pp. 66–67). As Merleau-Ponty writes, learning to see colours is 'the institution of a new dimension of experience', an opening of a whole field of possible experiences on the basis of an 'acquisition of a certain style of vision, a new use of one's own body' (Merleau-Ponty, 2012, pp. 32, 154–155). Child development should be understood as a 'reworking and renewal of the body schema' (ibid., 143), a 'progressive and discontinuous structuration (*Gestaltung, Neugestaltung*) of behaviour' (Merleau-Ponty, 1963, p. 177).

The subsequent categorisation of colours in language surely affects our perception in a top-down direction. However, this process can itself be understood only in a framework that clarifies our ability to reorganise perception through differentiation in the first place (cf. Merleau-Ponty, 2012, p. 154). In other words, the abstract conceptual super-structure may contribute to the reorganisation of our situation, but we cannot say that it assures this process originally and exclusively (cf. Woelert, 2011). Not only are hylemorphic explanations problematic here because they require one to introduce another factor linking the two dimensions together and thus lead to an infinite regress, more importantly, they do not accurately describe the structure of the dynamic dependence between experienced situations and our exploratory-behavioural activities.

Moreover, as Wertheimer's (1959) studies show, the process of differentiation of situation is to be found in domains beyond corporeal learning. Those pupils who only mechanically apply general mathematical rule to new cases are limited in their success rate by the conformity of the new cases to the cases used to demonstrate the rule. Inversely, a concrete case cannot enrich a general rule if it is not viewed as a variant of that rule in the first place. In contrast to that, those pupils who learned to solve the task to count the surface of a parallelogram *in all cases*, acquired the skill to restructure the initial situation (a given parallelogram) by changing the relationship between the situation as a whole, and its parts, for example by introducing auxiliary lines in the parallelogram (see ibid., pp. 13–58; cf. Merleau-Ponty, 2010, p. 55).[10] In other words, those who truly learned to solve this mathematical task became able to respond with a particular type of solution to a particular type of problem regardless of which concrete elements of the problem and of the solution were factually involved. This success lies beyond generalising and applying, because it requires becoming able to actively change the structure of a situation by reorganising it, that is, to transform one whole into another. What is learned is thus neither concrete nor general, it is rather a schema that organises the mutual relationships between what can be abstractly described as a general rule and concrete occurrences.

In general, the above considerations imply that we do not encounter 'new' situations blindly and 'unpredictably' as empiricist accounts suggest, but always as *variants* of our current norms of how to organise experiences which open a field of possible experiences. Inversely, 'here and now' situations never lead to learning *as individual experiences*, but only inasmuch as they are *normative*, that is, inasmuch as they represent some *type* of situation. In other words, we do not learn from particular contents of experience as opposed to an abstract form, concept or idea, but only from some contents inasmuch it instantiates a particularly organised whole.

Correspondingly, not all situations experienced 'first hand' lead to learning, but only those that relate to my current behavioural standards in the first place, and in addition have the quality of directing my exploratory capacities, such as my gaze, so as to require from us to use them differently. To learn then means to refine how we experientially organise *situations* by developing different types of *behaviours* by means of which we actively take a stand in regard to these situations.

The interpretation of learning as differentiation of experiential schemas moreover clarifies why learning is not 'seamless', linear and cumulative. Learning leads to non-linear revisions of our experience which have a retrospective effect (cf. Howell, 2015, pp. 332–333) and also prospectively open an infinite field of future experiences.[11] Learning does not consist in internalising a general rule of behaviour and then applying it to a particular case, or inversely in cumulatively producing the former from the latter by generalisation, or in a combination of both. It involves events of *global* reorganisation and it is only as such that knowledge thereby acquired is *universally transferable* and can be truly called learning.

Conclusion

A comprehensive theory of learning from experience requires us to simultaneously account for the facts that we learn on the basis of our concrete situation and that we learn something transferable to other situations. We have seen how Kant takes notice of these two aspects of experience by distinguishing an intuitively graspable matter and intelligible form of experience. As a consequence, however, he is forced to introduce the schematism, a principle guiding us in the process of relating the two aspects of experience that were distinguished.

Similarly to Kant, Kolb introduces the idea of four distinct experiential modes: concrete apprehension, abstract comprehension, action and observation. Consequently, Kolb defines learning as an interaction between these modes. However, he does not see the necessity of a principle similar to Kant's schematism and thus fails to explain concretely how the interaction is realised. Kolb's epistemological framework thus remains too abstract and the aspects of experiences that were separated by him are not accurately related. The idea of learning as a movement through a learning cycle lacks epistemological justification.

In order to demonstrate the excessively abstract character of Kolb's description of the experiential modes, we have examined Merleau-Ponty's phenomenological description of perception. Perception properly described does not fit to Kolb's concept of 'apprehension:' it is not a subjective event taking place in an individual experience and having the form of a direct contact with a reality given as an immediate fact. Rather, all perception is *mediated* by the *pre-personal* capacities of my body to *act* and this complex has a *general* value of a starting position for actions realised at different points of time and space, and potentially even by different individuals. An analysis of the example of perception confirms that all the elements that Kolb distinguishes as aspects of the 'learning cycle' are always structured by all the other elements.

Learning therefore cannot be defined as a transaction *between* distinct experiential modes separately providing concrete, abstract, observational and action-related experiences. A given situation has the potential to lead to learning not because it is now experienced 'first hand' as something that has never been experienced and therefore augments the field defined by an 'abstract' idea; rather, we learn something from a situation because it requires a systematic reorganisation of the schematic function on the basis of which it was accessed in the first place, because it requires an act of differentiation of our schemas. This account of learning also corresponds well to the fact that learning is not a cumulative, additive act, but a global redistribution of values of a situation. From this point of view, we are better situated to describe retrospective and prospective effects of learning, and the fact that it must be defined as leading to a universally transferrable experience.

Notes

1 Although Kant and various philosophers of mathematics have different opinions on this matter, algebraic and geometrical proofs are in fact realized by means of writing and drawing as instruments of evidencing (see Giaquinto, 2007 or Manoscu, 2008 on recent theories of 'instrumental practice' in mathematics). Plato denies this fact even though his own description of mathematical learning involves drawing (see *Meno*, Cooper and Hutchinson, 1997, pp. 880–886).

2 This is the opinion expressed for example by Peirce (Hartshorne and Weiss 1931, p. 15) and supported by Merleau-Ponty, who claims that the matter and form of experience 'must not be given an originary value' because they are merely 'the results of analysis' operated by the hylemorphic epistemology (2012, p. 251).

3 However, as, for example, Merleau-Ponty pointed out (2012, p. 241 note 61; 1963, pp. 129–137), Gestalt psychology loses the epistemological value of the *Gestalt* by interpreting it as a part of the physical world. Analogically, although the concept of schema has appeared in psychology and cognitive sciences (see Piaget, 1952; Ghosh and Gilboa, 2014), it was employed one-sidedly as a mere supplement of an intellectualist epistemological stance.

4 Strictly speaking, the Kantian approach leads to infinite regress because it requires one to introduce a supplementary mediating factor *at each next level* (cf. Champagne, 2018). Kant is himself touching on this problem when, apart

from the most general, transcendental schematism, he introduces also more concrete schemas of pure sensible and empirical concepts.

5 It is also significant that Kolb systematically refers to William James and other empiricist philosophers who accept the idea of a 'pure' sensorial experience (cf., e.g. Kolb, 2015, pp. 59, 70).

6 See Merleau-Ponty's discussion of 'motor habits' (2012, pp. 143–148) and 'perceptual habits' (ibid., pp. 153–155).

7 Merleau-Ponty refers to empirical research of his time (2012, pp. 216–221; commenting on this topic, Howell, 2015, p. 330, points to a more recent study, Schauss 1985). The original motor dimension of perception has been variously described also by Husserl (1997, pp. 131–170), Gibson (2014) or more recently enactivists (e.g. Noë, 2004; Sheets-Johnstone, 2011).

8 Cf. how for example Matherne (2016) justifies the use of the Kantian concept of schema in the context of Merleau-Ponty's account of perception.

9 Cf. Dreyfus (2002); He and Jespersen (2017); Howell (2015); Marratto (2012, pp. 66–77); Moya (2014); Talero (2006); Standal and Moe (2011); Standal (2016, pp. 40–45); Stolz (2015).

10 Further, cf. Merleau-Ponty (2010, pp. 50–57, 1973, pp. 115–129, 2012, pp. 403–415). Mathematical learning as a process of structuration of our pre-mathematical schemas has been recently theorized by the didactics expert Hejný (2011; Hejný, Slezáková and Jirotková, 2013).

11 Merleau-Ponty generalizes his interpretation of perception in terms of experiential norms to supra-perceptual domains with the help of the concept of 'institution' which makes these temporal aspects clearly visible (cf. 1970, pp. 39–45, 1973, pp. 115–129, 2002, 2010, 2012, pp. 403–415; for my own commentary on this topic, see Halák and Klouda, 2018, pp. 384–392).

Bibliography

Champagne, M. (2018). Kantian Schemata: A Critique Consistent with the Critique. *Philosphical Investigations*, 41(4), pp. 436–445.

Cooper, J. M. and Hutchinson, D. S., eds. (1997). *Plato: Complete Works*. Indianapolis: Hackett Publishing.

Dreyfus, H. (2002). Intelligence without Representation – Merleau-Ponty's Critique of Mental Representation. The Relevance of Phenomenology to Scientific Explanation. *Phenomenology and the Cognitive Sciences*, 1(4), pp. 367–383.

Gallagher, S. (2005). *How the Body Shapes the Mind*. Oxford: Clarendon Press.

Giaquinto, M. (2007). *Visual Thinking in Mathematics: An Epistemological Study*. Oxford: Oxford University Press.

Gibson, J. J. (2014). *The Ecological Approach to Visual Perception: Classic Edition*. Hove: Psychology Press.

Ghosh, V. and Gilboa, A. (2014). What is a Memory Schema? A Historical Perspective on Current Neuroscience Literature. *Neuropsychologia*, 53, pp. 104–114.

Halák, J. and Klouda, J. (2018). The Institution of Life in Gehlen and Merleau-Ponty: Searching for the Common Ground for the Anthropological Difference. *Human Studies*, 41(3), pp. 371–394.

Hanna, R. (2018). Kant's Theory of Judgment. In: Edward N. Zalta (ed.). *The Stanford Encyclopedia of Philosophy* (Winter 2018 Edition), https://plato.stanford.edu/archives/win2018/entries/kant-judgment/.

Hartshorne, Ch. and Weiss, P., eds. (1931). *Collected Papers of Charles Sanders Peirce, Volume I, Principles of Philosophy*. Cambridge: Harvard University Press.

He, J. and Jespersen, E. (2017). Habitual Learning as Being-in-the-World: On Merleau-Ponty and the Experience of Learning. *Frontiers of Philosophy in China*, 12(2), pp. 306–321.

Hainämaa, S. (2015). Anonymity and Personhood: Merleau-Ponty's Account of the Subject of Perception. *Continental Philosophy Review*, 48(2), pp. 123–142.

Hejný, M. (2011). The Process of Discovery in Teaching Focusing on Building Schemas. In: J. Novotná and H. Moraová (eds). *SEMT'11 Proceedings*. Prague: PedF UK v Praze, pp. 150–157.

Hejný, M., Slezáková, J. and Jirotková, D. (2013). Understanding Equations in Schema-oriented Education. *Procedia – Social and Behavioral Sciences*, 93, pp. 995–999.

Howell, W. (2015). Learning and the Development of Meaning: Husserl and Merleau-Ponty on the Temporality of Perception and Habit. *The Southern Journal of Philosophy*, 53(3), pp. 311–337.

Husserl, E. (1997). *Thing and Space. Lectures of 1907*. Dordrecht: Kluwer.

Husserl, E. (2013). *Cartesian Meditations: An Introduction to Phenomenology*. Dodrecht: Springer Science & Business Media.

Kant, I. (1999). *Critique of Pure Reason*. Cambridge: Cambridge University Press.

Kolb, D. A. (2015). *Experiential Learning: Experience as the Source of Learning and Development*. Upper Saddle River: FT Press.

Manoscu, P., ed. (2008). *The Philosophy of Mathematical Practice*. New York: Oxford University Press.

Marratto, S. L. (2012). *Intercorporeal Self, The: Merleau-Ponty on Subjectivity*. New York: Suny Press.

Matherne, S. (2016). Kantian Themes in Merleau-Ponty's Theory of Perception. *Archiv für Geschichte der Philosophie*, 98(2), pp. 193–230.

Merleau-Ponty, M. (1963). *Structure of Behavior*. Boston: Beacon Press.

Merleau-Ponty, M. (1968). *The Visible and the Invisible*. Evanston: Northwestern University Press.

Merleau-Ponty, M. (1970). *Themes from the Lectures*. Evanston: Northwestern University Press.

Merleau-Ponty, M. (1973). *Prose of the World*. Evanston: Northwestern University Press.

Merleau-Ponty, M. (2002). *Husserl at the Limits of Phenomenology*. Evanston: Northwestern University Press.

Merleau-Ponty, M. (2010). *Institution and Passivity: Course Notes from the Collège de France (1954–1955)*. Evanston: Northwestern University Press.

Merleau-Ponty, M. (2011). *Le monde sensible et le monde de l'expression*. Grenoble: MetissPress.

Merleau-Ponty, M. (2012). *Phenomenology of Perception*. London: Routledge.

Moya, P. (2014). Habit and Embodiment in Merleau-Ponty. *Habits: Plasticity, Learning and Freedom. Frontiers in Human Neuroscience*, 9, pp. 34–36.

Noë, A. (2004). *Action in Perception*. Cambridge: MIT Press.

Schauss, A. (1985). The Physiological Effect of Color on the Suppression of Human Aggression: Research on Baker-Miller Pink. *International Journal of Biosocial Research*, 7(2), pp. 55–64.

Sheets-Johnstone, M. (2011). *The Primacy of Movement*. Amsterdam: John Benjamins Publishing.

Standal, Ø. (2016). *Phenomenology and Pedagogy in Physical Education*. London: Routledge.

Standal, Ø. F. and Moe, V. F. (2011). Merleau-Ponty Meets Kretchmar: Sweet Tensions of Embodied Learning. *Sport, Ethics and Philosophy*, 5(3), pp. 256–269.

Stolz, S. A. (2015). Embodied Learning. *Educational Philosophy and Theory*, 47(5), pp. 474–487.

Talero, M. (2006). Merleau-Ponty and the Bodily Subject of Learning. *International Philosophical Quarterly*, 46(2), pp. 191–203.

Wertheimer, M. (1959). *Productive Thinking*. New York: Harper.

Woelert, P. (2011). Human Cognition, Space, and the Sedimentation of Meaning. *Phenomenology and the Cognitive Sciences*, 10(1), pp. 113–137.

6 John Dewey's conceptualisation of experience

John Quay

Experience and outdoor education

A signature contribution that outdoor education makes to the theory and practice of education more broadly is the positioning of experience as central to learning, indeed *as* learning. Much of this work has been encapsulated under the umbrella of 'experiential learning' that gained prominence among outdoor educators in the 1970s (Seaman, Brown and Quay, 2017). While many education disciplines – for example mathematics education, science education and history education – emphasise content knowledge and pedagogical content knowledge (Shulman, 1986) as the major foci for learning and teaching practice, outdoor education explicitly strives to work educationally with the experiences of participants.

This isn't to say that experience does not figure in the discourses surrounding other education disciplines. The notion of pedagogical content knowledge draws attention to 'the ways of representing and formulating the subject [matter] that make it comprehensible to others' (Shulman, 1986, 6–7). Thus, the focus is not only content knowledge per se, but includes the ways in which a teacher designs encounters between students and content such that comprehension is achievable. The emphasis here, however, remains encapsulated within what are perceived to be the two primary elements believed to exhaustively describe education, leaving no room for other considerations: curriculum (understood as content) and pedagogy (understood as teaching method), also paired as content and process, or subject-matter and method.

The emphasis in outdoor education is different, but it does not discount knowledge. The nature of this difference can be seen by following Shulman in the direction indicated by pedagogical content knowledge, where the comprehension of others is highlighted. Outdoor education seeks to work with the experiences of these others, acknowledging more explicitly that they have biographies, individual but shared biographies, that are constantly being written, made, constructed and performed. This is a reversal of emphasis, positioning knowledge within experiences, thereby highlighting how experiences are more foundational educationally than pedagogy and curriculum. Such a reversal recognises that content is contextualised within method, and both are contextualised meaningfully within experiences, as experiences.

John Dewey was a philosopher of education who similarly believed in 'an intimate and necessary relation between the processes of actual experience and education' (1938, 20). An obvious requirement for applying this understanding is 'having a correct idea of experience'. Much of his voluminous oeuvre contributes to this quest 'for a sound philosophy of experience' (1938, 90). And as Pascucci (2016, 1) avers, 'nearly a hundred years later, the project is still in progress'.

Outdoor educators, and others writing with educative outdoor experiences in mind, have drawn on Dewey's ideas in order to forward the development of educational theory, often under the banner of experiential learning, in support of pedagogical practices employed in outdoor education and other outdoor learning situations. Recently, building on his long-term engagement with Dewey's work, Thorburn (2018, 27) has argued that 'there remains a need to review the conceptual ideas of thinkers (such as Dewey) whose theorizing continues to influence outdoor educators'. As this project has progressed, and continues to progress, various conceptualisations of experiential learning have been forwarded and problematised (Seaman, Brown and Quay, 2017). Seaman (2008, 4) has been at the forefront of a growing number who have critiqued simplistic representations of experiential learning as a psychological cycle, where particular aspects of Dewey's work are often called upon to theoretically substantiate such 'stepwise models'. Ord and Leather also speak to this issue, drawing a distinction between the stepwise models and Dewey's endeavours. They claim that, 'at the heart of the differences between, on the one hand, Dewey's theory of experiential learning ... and on the other the popularised simplistic learning cycle is the conceptualisation of experience itself' (Ord and Leather, 2011, 17).

It is this conceptualisation of experience itself that remains in question, building on Dewey's (1938, 30) 'idea that a coherent *theory* of experience, affording positive direction to selection and organisation of appropriate educational methods and materials, is required by the attempt to give new direction to the work of the schools'. Dewey never clearly articulated this coherent theory of experience, leading to a situation where 'Dewey's thinking on experiential-informed education has been regularly criticized for being rather scattered, vague on detail and inconsistent' (Thorburn and Allison, 2017, 107). Yet Dewey himself claimed, in the twilight of his career, that 'with respect to the hanging together of various problems and various hypotheses in a perspective determined by a definite point of view, I have a system' (1940, 244). This suggests that while Dewey's ideas may be scattered throughout his many published writings, coherence is access-ible. It is my aim in this chapter to put forward an interpretation that coheres multiple facets of Dewey's work on experience and education. But rather than provide a mere exposition of Dewey's philosophy, I shall also dialogue with another interpretation of Dewey's philosophy of education argued by educational philosopher R. S. Peters (1977).

According to Pring (2007, 4), Peters 'gives a sympathetic but ultimately critical account' of Dewey's philosophy. The sympathetic aspects of Peters' account provide a positive rendering of the connection Dewey makes between experience and education. However, Peters' positive account is accompanied by the identification of issues he has with aspects of Dewey's philosophy, opening the door to further debate. Initially I shall engage with Peters' more general statements on Dewey's philosophy, offered in the introduction to his chapter, in order to provide an overview of Dewey's conception of experience. In doing so I shall draw together various ways in which Dewey speaks of experience in order to highlight the coherence across these.

Following this I shall provide a version of Peters' positive account and then explore his criticisms, many of which stem from the challenge of addressing the coherency of Dewey's views. This will enable me to intro-duce a more coherent interpretation of Dewey's philosophy of experience and education. This perspective brings Dewey's understanding of aesthetic experience, which I argue that Peters overlooked, into functional relation with his work in logic, or reflective experience. Such an interpretation may hopefully advance a little further the project of articulating a sound philo-sophy of experience that Dewey engaged with many years ago, helping to further inform various understandings of experiential learning and outdoor education.

An overview of Dewey's conception of experience

In the introduction to his chapter, Peters (1977, 65) identified what he believed to be 'the key to understanding Dewey's philosophy of educa-tion', which is 'the realization that he was, for a long time, a Hegelian who later became converted to Pragmatism'. This perspective on Dewey's intellectual development is captured in an autobiographical statement pub-lished in 1930, titled 'From absolutism to experimentalism'. Here Dewey acknowledged that his development was 'controlled largely by a struggle between a native inclination toward the schematic and formally logical, and those incidents of personal experience that compelled me to take account of actual material' (1930, 16). The struggle between these two positions was expressed in Dewey's penchant for 'getting rid of dualisms' (Peters, 1977, 65), an urge for unification that he drew from Hegel's absolutism. Peters provides evidence for this by quoting the titles of major works by Dewey in education, with the 'and' in each title denoting the move to unification: *The school and society* (1900), *The child and the curriculum* (1902), *Interest and effort in education* (1913), *Democracy and education* (1916a), *Experience and education* (1938).

This unification was achieved for Dewey via his 'logical version of pragmatism' (1916b, 331), which built on Peirce's pragmatic principle: 'the meaning of terms, propositions, and arguments or reasoned inference, of ideas and trains of ideas, is always found in the *consequences*, in the practical effects to which they lead' (Dewey, 1935, 338). Pragmatism yields a unification of theory and practice; but how to work with it? In responding to Peirce's maxim, Dewey sought 'the construction of a logic, that is, a method of effective inquiry' (1930, 23). In language more closely aligned with education he described this logic as 'the theory of the method of knowing' which 'may be termed pragmatic' because 'its essential feature is to maintain the continuity of knowing with an activity which purposely modifies the environment' (1916a, 400). Dewey positioned this logic, this theory of inquiry, as reflective thinking, or more broadly as reflective experience; summarising the 'general features of a reflective experience' as:

i   perplexity, confusion, doubt, due to the fact that one is implicated in an incomplete situation whose full character is not yet determined;

ii   a conjectural anticipation – a tentative interpretation of the given elements, attributing to them a tendency to effect certain consequences;

iii   a careful survey (examination, inspection, exploration, analysis) of all attainable consideration which will define and clarify the problem in hand;

iv   a consequent elaboration of the tentative hypothesis to make it more precise and more consistent, because squaring with a wider range of facts;

v   taking one stand upon the projected hypothesis as a plan of action which is applied to the existing state of affairs: doing something overtly to bring about the anticipated result, and thereby testing the hypothesis.

(Dewey, 1916a, 176)

While the numbered items above may appear like a stepwise recipe, Dewey (1933, 115) was clear that these 'functions of thought ... do not follow one another in set order'. Testimony to this claim is his identification of 'two types' of reflective experience, differentiated 'according to the proportion of reflection found in them'. The first type he equated with 'the method of trial and error': 'we simply do something, and when it fails, we do something else, and keep on trying till we hit upon something that works, and then we adopt that method as a rule of thumb measure in subsequent procedure' (Dewey, 1916a, 177). This method ignores (iii) and (iv) above, highlighting for Dewey how 'it is the extent and accuracy of steps three and four which mark of a distinctive reflective experience from one on the trial and error plane' (1916a, 176). And yet, true to the pragmatic maxim, steps three and four cannot be disconnected from other functions of thought. 'We never get wholly beyond the trial and error situation', Dewey argued.

> Our most elaborate and rationally consistent thought has to be tried in the world and thereby tried out. And since it can never take into account all the connections [applicable to a problem], it can never cover with perfect accuracy all the consequences.
>
> (1916a, 177)

This relation between trial and error reflective experience and distinctive reflective experience sits at the heart of Dewey's logical version of pragmatism.

Being a logic of inquiry, Dewey spoke of reflective experience in connection with a problem and its resolution. It is this that Peters (1977, 65) seized on in his interpretation of Dewey's philosophy of education, asserting that 'his philosophy, it might be said, was an attempt to introduce into this new institution [the school] the problem-solving, do-it-yourself method of the learning of his boyhood'; this along with 'the close link between learning and living and the sense of contributing to a social whole permeated by shared experiences'.

This emphasis on problem-solving is one Peters will eventually raise as a chief concern with Dewey's philosophy of education. I shall expand on this concern in the latter parts of this chapter, however it is important to mention at this point that reflective experience does not comprise the whole of Dewey's philosophy of experience. There is a further understanding of experience, signaled in the account of reflective experience above but not highlighted. This understanding is illuminated by Dewey's claim that there are 'two limits of every unit of [reflective] thinking': 'a perplexed, troubled or confused situation at the beginning and a cleared-up, unified, resolved situation at the close' (1933, 106). At the beginning the situation is '*pre*-reflective'; and at the close the situation is '*post*-reflective' (1933, 107). So just what is this 'non-reflective' (1916b, 137fn) experience?

The major expression of this non-reflective experience is held in Dewey's (1934) book *Art as experience*. It is worth noting the use of 'as' in the title rather than 'and', in that Dewey was not attempting to unify art and experience by bringing them together functionally via his logical version of pragmatism. Instead, his task this time is 'that of recovering the continuity of aesthetic experience with normal processes of living' (1934, 10), those 'everyday events, doings, and sufferings that are universally recognized to constitute experience' (1934, 3). Dewey considers ordinary everyday experiences to be chiefly aesthetic, not reflective.

> For aesthetic experience is experience in its integrity. Had not the term 'pure' been so often abused in philosophic literature, had it not been so often employed to suggest that there is something alloyed, impure, in the very nature of experience and to denote something beyond experience, we might say that aesthetic experience is pure experience. For it is experience freed from the forces that impede and confuse its development as experience; freed, that is, from factors that subordinate an experience as it is directly had to something beyond itself. To aesthetic experience, then, the philosopher must go to understand what experience is.
>
> (1934, 274)

The meaning of 'aesthetic' as an adjective, when applied to experience, refers to the act 'of perception and "enjoyment"' (Dewey, 1934, 46), highlighting basic perceptive experience and its emotive character. To acknowledge aesthetic experience is to be aware of experience as chiefly unproblematic, characterised emotionally in ways that do not engender reflective experience. Reflective experience then originates in aesthetic experience that is emotional in a way that highlights some felt 'perplexity, confusion, doubt' (1916a, 176). Therefore, 'experience is emotional, but there are no separate things called emotions in it' (1934, 42). Aesthetic experience is emotional, but to see separate emotions is to engage in reflective experience.

Hence, in the coherence of Dewey's theory of experience, experience has within it two emphases. 'The difference between the aesthetic and the intellectual is ... one of the places where emphasis falls in the constant rhythm' of experience, a rhythm 'that marks the interaction of the live creature with his [*sic*] surroundings' (1934, 15). It is this rhythm of emphasis within experience – aesthetic and reflective – which is in play in Dewey's 'technical definition of education' as that 'reconstruction or reorganization of [pre-reflective aesthetic] experience [via reflective experience] which adds to the meaning of [aesthetic] experience, and which increases ability to direct the course of subsequent [post-reflective aesthetic] experience' (1916a, 89–90). This definition embraces the notion that aesthetic experience – as everyday, ordinary, unproblematic experience – is the foundation that reflective experience supports by enabling change in aesthetic experience, as learning. In this sense, reflective experience is also aesthetic, but aesthetic experience is not reflective. Reflective experience is emotional in a way connected with the situation that gave rise to it, but not the other way around. Expressed in Dewey's words, 'aesthetic [experience] cannot be sharply marked off from intellectual experience since the latter must bear an aesthetic stamp to be itself complete' (1934, 38).

It is ordinary aesthetic experiences 'directly had' (Dewey, 1934, 274) by those participating that form the source of the educational content for outdoor education. It is within such aesthetic experience that problems emerge requiring reflective experience for their resolution. The rhythmic relation between aesthetic and reflective experience points to how knowledge is not only content but, as knowing, is embedded within aesthetic experience and expressed through habituated practices, through ways of doing which have been arrived at via previous learning episodes to be embedded within aesthetic experience. Knowing is contextualised in doing, in process, and both are meaningfully contextualised within being. All three – being–doing–knowing – are submerged within aesthetic experience (for further explication see Quay, 2013, 2015). But they can, of course, be separated in reflective experience, to reveal their connections in the form of what Dewey calls an occupation.

Occupations, for Dewey, are not just adult jobs, distributed one per adult. Instead, every person, no matter what their age, has 'a variety of callings' (1916a, 359). Hence Dewey spoke against vocational education. 'Nothing could be more absurd than to try to educate individuals with an eye to only one line of activity' (1916a, 359). The biography of a career may reveal several jobs, yet it shows many more occupations; and a life shows many, many more. The complexity of life can be understood in this way: via the many occupations that interact and intersect at different times and places. For example, 'no one is just an artist and nothing else', Dewey (1916a, 359) argued, for an artist 'must, at some period of his [*sic*] life, be a member of a family; he must have friends and companions; he must either support himself or be supported by others, ... and so on'. An occupation is a way of being–doing–knowing: being a family member, being a friend, being a dependent, being a parent, being a student, being a gardener, being a swimmer, being a commuter: a never-ending list. We are always already living some occupation, but we rarely stop to name it. And naming an occupation never really captures the nuance of the experience of being occupied in such a way.

Occupations are central to the connection Dewey sees between experience and education. In educational terms, Dewey (1900, 131) defined an 'occupation' as 'a mode of activity on the part of the child which reproduces or runs parallel to, some form of work carried on in social life'. In fact, he declared that 'education *through* occupations ... combines within itself more of the factors conducive to learning than any other method' (1916a, 361). It is with occupations that the relation Dewey saw between experience and education becomes most intimate.

Peters' sympathetic account of Dewey's philosophy of education

Peters also paid heed to Dewey's work on occupations. He was aware that, during the early decades of the twentieth century when Dewey was writing about occupations, the idea of vocational education was taking root, which Dewey 'deprecated' because it encouraged a 'split between the practical and the liberal which reflected an undesirable type of class-structure' (Peters, 1977, 71). Rather than creating two different types of school, one for trades and the other for academic work, Dewey was attempting, via occupations, to infuse all schools with curriculum and pedagogy which would draw on pragmatism as an underlying philosophy, arguing 'that if more practical activities were introduced into schools, education would be *through* occupations and not *for* occupations' (Peters, 1977, 71).

However, this argument should not be misconstrued as one placing the needs of the child somehow above and beyond curriculum content – recall occupations as being–doing–knowing. 'Dewey is sometimes classified with those progressives who have extolled following the interests of the child at the expense of subject-matter', Peters points out (Peters, 1977, 70). Yet 'this is completely to misunderstand his position, for he was too much of a Hegelian to ignore the importance of a society's "cultural heritage" which he described as "the ripe fruitage of experience"' Peters (1977, 70).

But while Dewey was adamant that subject-matter was integral, he did not prescribe curriculum as content per se, instead viewing curriculum through the lens of occupation: as (being–doing–)knowing, via his theory of knowing, rather than just as knowledge. In the revised edition of *The school and society* (1915, originally published 1900) he devoted a chapter to 'The psychology of occupations'. Here he made clear that 'the fundamental point in the psychology of an occupation is that it maintains a balance between the intellectual and the practical phases of experience' (131), where these are the two types of reflective experience.

Peters rightfully declares that 'most of what Dewey wrote about the curriculum related to the elementary school and much of it seems rather dated' (Peters, 1977, 70). Drawing on occupations, Dewey 'stressed ... the importance of practical activities such as sewing, cooking, weaving, carpentry and metalwork' which 'were basic to life' (70). These occupations were simplistically applied as the source of curriculum in the University of Chicago's Elementary School, with Dewey arguing that they would 'not only recapitulate past important activities of the race, but reproduce those of the child's present environment' (1915, originally published 1900, 136). Such an understanding of occupations has been rightly discredited because 'influenced by the presiding ethnocentric and imperialistic views' (Fallace, 2012, 511), highlighting how teachers, with educational aims and responsibilities, must critically engage with occupations in an ethical sense.

For Dewey, such critical educational engagement must be around 'the selection of orderly and continuous modes of occupation', highlighting 'the problem ... of discovering and arranging the occupations' (1933, 51–52):

a   that are most congenial, best adapted, to the immature stage of development;
b   that have the most ulterior promise as preparation for the social responsibilities of adult life; and
c   that, *at the same time*, have the maximum of influence in forming habits as acute observation and of consecutive inference.

(Dewey, 1933, 52)

Occupations as being–doing–knowing are the stepping stones that biographically express the complex pathways through life, and not just life after school. 'Thus, education is not necessarily a matter of age; for education means the enterprise of supplying the conditions which ensure growth, or adequacy of life, irrespective of age' (Peters, 1977, 66). Occupations always play an educational role, be they within school or without. And they are not mere individual achievements, for as modes of social life, they impact the character of a society. It is because of this connection between education and society that Dewey argued for 'a measure for the worth of any given mode of social life' (1916a, 96), citing 'two elements' which 'both point to democracy' (1916a, 100).

The first signifies not only more numerous and more varied points of shared common interest, but greater reliance upon the recognition of mutual interests as a factor in social control. The second means not only freer interaction between social groups ... but change in social habit – its continuous readjustment through meeting the new situations produced by varied intercourse. And these two traits are precisely what characterize the democratically constituted society.

(Dewey, 1916a, 100)

These criteria enabled Dewey to put forward some counter examples for occupations. As Peters indicates, Dewey argued against certain forms of occupation based on his understanding of education as growth, for 'growth in efficiency as a burglar, as a gangster, or as a corrupt politician does not lead to further growth'. This sense of growth is, according to Peters, 'taken from biology'; or perhaps more broadly, from Darwin's work on evolution (Dewey, 1910). Significantly, 'it enabled him to argue that growth, properly understood, can only flourish in a democratic environment' (Peters, 1977, 66–68).

A teacher's task is thus a difficult one, a complex one, because a human one; and it is in this sense a never-ending one: 'an endless circle or spiral' (Dewey, 1929, 77). Dewey understood this, declaring that 'there is no way to discover what *is* "more truly educational"' in any finished sense; instead, what is more educational must be striven for 'by the continuation of the educational act itself. The discovery is never made; it is always making' (Dewey, 1929, 76–77). It is for this reason that Dewey's attempts at defining curriculum in the University Elementary School were exploratory and not prescriptive. In addition, and as Peters acknowledges, Dewey 'was always very guarded about details of teaching methods. He confined himself to generalities, knowing that details of implementation must vary with individuals' (Peters, 1977, 69). Any attempt at a complete answer for curriculum and pedagogy 'arrests growth' rather than supporting it, because 'it prevents the thinking that is the final source of all progress' (Dewey, 1929, 77).

Peters' critical account of Dewey's philosophy of education

As stated earlier, it is my aim in this chapter to put forward an interpretation that brings together multiple facets of Dewey's work on experience and education, and in this way to approach a coherent understanding of Dewey's conceptualisation of experience. More than this, though, I am drawing on Peters 'sympathetic but ultimately critical account' (Pring, 2007, 4) of Dewey's philosophy of education in order to raise Peters' positive considerations of Dewey's philosophy, as described in the previous section, and also his concerns. Responding to these concerns enables me to achieve a more deeply considered interpretation of Dewey's philosophy of education, and his conceptualisation of experience, than achievable through a mere exposition.

Being educated

Key among Peters' concerns is Dewey's reliance on pragmatism as the underpinning philosophy which knits together the many dualisms he perceives splitting education. 'In putting forward an ideal which is meant to resolve current dualisms', Peters argues that Dewey developed 'a very one-sided view of man [*sic*] that completely ignores certain features of the human condition' (1977, 75). Peters focuses his 'criticisms' on Dewey's 'account of the "growth" of the problem-solving man [*sic*]' (1977, 72), also referring more expansively to 'Dewey's ideal of the technological, problem-solving man [*sic*]'. According to Peters, this technological, problem-solving version 'is central' to understanding Dewey's 'convictions about the methods and content of education and his conception of democracy'. Everything about Dewey's philosophy of education and its relationship with experience, for Peters, is tied up with this conception of 'the human condition' (1977, 75). And it sits at the heart of Peters' disquiet.

Underpinning Peters' criticisms is his own conceptual analysis of 'Education and the Educated Man [*sic*]' (1970a), and how to achieve this idea of 'being educated'. He clearly states that 'processes of education ... are those that lead up to the development of an educated person', while also acknowledging, perhaps with traces of Dewey's notion of growth, that 'there is no end to this process' (1973, 20).

> Education ... can have no ends beyond itself. Its value derives from principles and standards implicit in it. To be educated is not to have arrived at a destination; it is to travel with a different view. What is required is not feverish preparation for something that lies ahead, but to work with precision, passion and taste at worth-while things that lie to hand. These worth-while things cannot be forced on reluctant minds, neither are they flowers towards which the seeds of mentality develop in the sun of the teacher's smile. They are acquired by contact with those who have already acquired them and who have patience, zeal, and competence enough to *initiate* others into them.
>
> (Peters, 1965, 110, italics added)

While it may seem that there are parallels visible here in the conceptions of education held by Peters and Dewey, these parallels don't extend very far. The differences become more obvious when process is made the focus. Peters draws heavily on the notion of initiation to convey his comprehension of the process of education; the quotation above is from a chapter titled 'Education as initiation' (1965). Another chapter with the same title but not the same content appears in his book *Ethics and education* wherein he claims that 'education consists essentially in the initiation of members of a society into a form of life that is thought to be worthwhile' (1970b, 237). Such worthwhile forms of life reflect subjects or studies in the school curriculum. They are 'differentiated modes of thought and awareness ... characterized both by a content or 'body of knowledge' and by public procedures by means of which this content has been accumulated, criticized, and revised' (Peters, 1970b, 50); for example, 'science, history, mathematics, religious and aesthetic awareness, together with moral, prudential and technical forms of thought and action'. Significantly, Peters claims that 'the process of initiation into such modes of thought and awareness is the process of education' (1970b, 51).

How initiation happens is a further question. Peters sees benefit in 'authoritarian methods of education' espoused by 'traditional teachers', as well as the methods of 'growth-theorists' who argue that 'being educated implies interest in and care for what is worth-while'. However, Peters does not fully concur with the arguments of the growth-theorists, such as Dewey, mainly because he believes that they sidestep a conviction held by traditional teachers: 'that education involves the intentional transmission of worth-while content' (1965, 96–97). In other words, worthwhile content does not necessarily have to be of interest to, or have relevance in, the present life of a young person; for, says Peters, with a reproachful nod to pragmatism, 'contributing to practical purposes is only one criterion of "relevance"' (1977, 76). Peters believes that while children may not presently consider some forms of life worth-while, 'once they get started on them they will eventually come to care. They will thus emerge as educated men [*sic*]' (1965, 96).

Initiation versus interest

These discrepancies between Dewey and Peters, expressed in connection with the process of education – Dewey (1913) arguing for interest and Peters for initiation – beg a further level of examination: achievable via juxtaposition of Dewey's notion of occupations with Peters' idea of forms of life. For Peters, the origin of education is with a worth-while form of life as a mode of thought and awareness, characterised as a body of knowledge, which a person is then initiated into, to eventually emerge as an educated person. Knowing is primary in this understanding of education.

Knowing contextualises doing, as the process of knowing; and both contextualise the achievement of being an educated person: knowing–doing–being. However for Dewey, as mentioned earlier, the contextual relations are the opposite. Knowing is contextualised in doing, in process, and both are meaningfully contextualised within being: being–doing–knowing (see Figure 6.1). All three are occupational, emphasising the points made earlier that occupations are not just adult jobs, and one is never not engaged in some occupation.

As knowing, an occupation is 'an organizing principle for information and ideas; for knowledge and intellectual growth', providing 'an axis which runs through an immense diversity of detail; it causes different experiences, facts, items of information to fall into order with one another'. As doing, an occupation is 'a continuous activity having a purpose' (Dewey, 1916a, 362). Both knowing and doing are occupational. But even more importantly, because pointing to aesthetic experience, Dewey argued that 'active occupations should be concerned primarily with *wholes*' (232). And 'wholes for purposes of education are not … physical affairs' as in a collection of separate but related things, such as things in a classroom. 'Intellectually', because connected with knowing, 'the existence of a whole depends upon a concern or interest; it is qualitative, the completeness of appeal made by a situation' (232). In other words, this qualitative, emotional whole of aesthetic experience *is* continuous activity having a purpose, *is* organising principle for information and ideas. Yet all are submerged within aesthetic experience, able to be separated in reflective experience. Interest is central because it also spans both aesthetic and reflective experience. In a comment that raises echoes of both aesthetic and reflective experience, Dewey asserted that 'interest marks the annihilation of the distance between the person and the materials and results of his action; it is the sign of their organic union' (1913, 17).

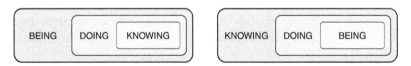

Figure 6.1 The different contextualizing relations of experience and education. On the left is that aligned with Dewey's conception of occupations as interest, where being is the most foundational. On the right is that aligned with Peters' conception of education as initiation to being educated, where knowing is the most foundational, held in bodies of knowledge.

Pragmatism is not aesthetic experience

Peters did not, to my knowledge, admit awareness of Dewey's under-standing of aesthetic experience or its rhythmic relation with reflective experience. The text *Art as experience* (1934) is central to a broader and more coherent comprehension of Dewey's theory of experience, yet it is a text to which Peters, as far as I can tell, does not refer. Commenting on criticisms received about this book, Dewey made a series of emphatic statements that differentiated aesthetic and reflective experience. 'I ... did *not* write *Art as Experience* as an appendix to or application of my prag-matism', he states (1948, 208). 'The actual fact is that I have consistently treated the pragmatic theory as a theory of *knowing*, and as confined within the limits of the field of specifically cognitive subject-matter'. And 'I have specifically rejected the idea that aesthetic subject-matter is a form of knowledge' (1948, 207–208); a point that highlights the submerged emo-tional character of aesthetic experience.

So, while a major underpinning of Peters' critique of Dewey's philo-sophy of education is his focus on the 'defects of the pragmatic stance' (1977, 76), Dewey's coherent theory of experience is not only pragmatic. Peters narrowly circumscribes Dewey's theory of experience within prag-matism, his logical version of pragmatism, without acknowledging how reflective experience is founded in ordinary, everyday aesthetic experi-ence. As a consequence, Peters does not perceive the 'rhythm' of emphasis within experience that Dewey (1934, 15) described as involving both 'the aesthetic and the intellectual'.

And acknowledgement of aesthetic experience defrays further criti-cisms. Peters argues that 'Dewey ... appreciated the importance of habit in life, but accorded no value to anything that was a matter of routine' (1977, 76). Peters also contends that 'there are ... the more distanced, aesthetic enjoyments that have little to do with problem-solving', charg-ing Dewey with 'neglect of the personal and of the education of the emo-tions' and as someone who 'sees nature just as something that can be used for human purposes' and thus lacking 'a sense of awe and of wonder' (1977, 76).

In short, Peters is concerned that if life is deemed purely pragmatic, then much that is important is excluded from consideration or considered in a narrowly practical way; an interpretation of 'practical' which Dewey actually denigrated, calling it 'a hard, narrow, and merely 'practical' prac-tice' (1916a, 161). Peters is thus of the position that being educated does not emerge via problem-solving alone, as there are many unproblematic moments in life, including aesthetic enjoyments, which do not engage reflective experience. In addition, 'there are many aspects of life ... that present not problems that can be solved but predicaments that have to be lived with' (1977, 76). Living with predicaments and other aspects of life's routine does not directly engage problem-solving but is still experience: aesthetic experience.

Unproblematic routine occurs as ordinary, everyday aesthetic experience, characterised emotionally as whole, but not replete with reflection. Such routine is able to occur without problems because relevant problems have been previously resolved to the extent that aesthetic experience is, in such moments, sufficiently intelligent. Dewey made a distinction 'between knowledge as the outcome of special inquiries (undertaken because of the presence of problems) and *intelligence* as the product and expression of cumulative funding of the meanings reached in these special cases' (1939, 521). Hence knowledge is recognised as an explicit product of reflective experience but submerged within aesthetic experience as meanings: which 'constitute *intelligence* when actually applied in new experiences' (1939, 564). This belies the 'opposition … said to exist between the intellect and the emotions', wherein 'the emotions are conceived to be purely private and personal, having nothing to do with the work of pure intelligence in apprehending facts and truths, – except perhaps the single emotion of intellectual curiosity' (1916a, 390–391). Such intelligent aesthetic experience may still involve what Peters calls predicaments, yet as 'predicaments that have to be lived with' (1977, 76), they stamp aesthetic experience emotionally, but not in a way which engenders reflective experience, at least in these moments.

Occupations and relevance

In making these criticisms, Peters asserts that 'the school, surely, should not concern itself only with what is relevant to contemporary problems' because 'it should also distance itself a bit from these and introduce children to speculations about the world in science, and to insights into the human condition in literature and history, which are of perennial significance' (1977, 72). In other words, 'to represent scientific theories, which are some of the greatest products of the human imagination, just as aids to action, is to ignore a whole dimension of human life' (1977, 76). And likewise, 'literature is singularly unamenable to the problem-solving method of learning, and often concerns itself with the predicaments of man rather than with his problems' (1977, 75). Such claims, as mentioned earlier, are underpinned by Peters' understanding of education as a process of initiation into worth-while forms of life as modes of thought and awareness having a specifiable body of knowledge, all of which seem to align well with school subjects.

These criticisms can be responded to if the broader coherence of Dewey's conception of experience – involving aesthetic and reflective experience as well as an understanding of how occupations underpin these emphases in experience – is acknowledged.

The challenge educationally is the difficulty posed by the issue of relevance. As mentioned earlier, Peters is willing to overlook the growth-theorist's insistence on the need to work with the present relevance of knowledge for young people, when teaching bodies of knowledge associated with worth-while forms of life. As a consequence, he is happy to support the employ of traditional methods of teaching when subject matter cannot (conceivably) be made practically relevant in the lives of young people.

But of course, relevance is still in play in traditional teaching. On the one hand, it is the relevance of these bodies of knowledge to adults that positions them as worth-while educationally. One aspect of this can be seen through the occupation of being a secondary school teacher, which is normally associated with expertise in particular school subjects. The bodies of knowledge held within these school subjects are thus of vital occupational significance to the teacher. On the other hand, some form of relevance for young people must still be addressed. This knowledge has to be relevant in some present way, for some present purpose, in some present occupation, otherwise it is meaningless.

Such relevance is traditionally supplied through discipline and assessment designed to engender in the child the occupation of the good student. As seen by the traditional teacher, 'the child is simply the immature-being who is to be matured: ... the superficial being who is to be deepened'; one whose 'narrow experience ... is to be widened' and who should merely 'receive' and 'accept'; whose 'part is fulfilled when ... ductile and docile' (Dewey, 1902, 8). So, when there is 'depreciation of interest' in an educational situation – when there is no present relevance perceived by young people of the content directly taught – this engenders 'the necessity in practice, with most pupils, of recourse to extraneous and irrelevant rewards and penalties' (1916a, 391). Hence 'the spectacle of professional educators decrying appeal to interest while they uphold with great dignity the need of reliance upon examinations, marks, promotions and demotions, prizes, and the time-honoured paraphernalia of rewards and punishments' (1916a, 391). Thus, one form of interest replaces another, bringing about the ubiquitous school-based occupation of the good student.

For Dewey, interest is occupation, as being–doing–knowing, meaning that an individual is always already involved in some socially recognised and understood occupation, while interpreting that involvement individually, or personally. From Dewey's perspective, 'an occupation is the only thing which balances the distinctive capacity of an individual with his social service' (1916a, 360). Occupations do not neglect the personal, for a person does not navigate a personal/public distinction but a continuing rhythm of aesthetic and reflective experience engaging both individual and social at the same time.

Such interpretation, orientated towards involvement in an occupation, can be applied beyond that occupation, between occupations, but always from the perspective of a particular occupation. One is always already involved in an occupation and therefore it is not possible to decide to sit outside any and every occupation, for doing this sets up a further occupation, ad infinitum. This enables selective decisions to be made concerning occupations. Awareness of different occupations, as being–doing–knowing, suggests that knowing and doing in one occupation may have different meaning in another occupation. This can position one occupation, interpreted from the perspective of another occupation, as irrational. Peters argues that Dewey's philosophy of education harbours a 'disregard of the irrational', which he directs 'against Dewey's confident reformist optimism' (1977, 76). In making this point, Peters acknowledges 'the view that civilization is a brittle crust containing with difficulty irrational yearnings' (1977, 76). Yet Dewey's philosophy does consider this issue.

While he sought a coherent theory of experience via which to comprehend education, Dewey did not claim that all particular experiences were positively educative in an ethical sense. His belief that 'all genuine education comes about through experiences does not mean that all experiences are genuinely or equally educative' (1938, 25). In fact, in this sense of particular experiences, he argued that 'experience and education cannot be directly equated to each other. For some experiences are mis-educative', meaning that a particular experience can arrest or distort the growth of further experiences. This understanding draws on occupations. 'A man, for example, who starts out on a career of burglary may grow in that direction, and by practice may grow into a highly expert burglar' (1938, 36). Yet from the standpoint of growth as education and education as growth the question is whether growth in this direction promotes or retards growth in general' (1938, 36). In other words, ethical questions always sit over experience when considered educationally. Such questions can be responded to via Dewey's two measures of the 'worth of any given mode of social life' (1916a, 96), both of which point to the interaction between occupations. As mentioned previously, the first focuses on 'more numerous and more varied points of shared common interest' (100) across occupations; the second emphasises 'freer interaction between social groups', leading to changes in occupations driven by such interaction. For Dewey, both of these occupational occurrences were best achieved via a 'demo-cratically constituted society'.

Conclusion

The positioning of outdoor education outside formal school curriculum is often considered a disadvantage, mainly because, employing Peters' philosophical position, outdoor education is not worth-while enough, as a form of life, to be included. This is then articulated more specifically in terms of its status as a discipline in connection with a relevant body of knowledge. Such a situation has played out in Australia over the past decade in connection with moves to develop an Australian curriculum (Martin, 2010).

Yet outdoor education does have a significant offering to make to the theory and practice of education more broadly, including those subjects that are expressed in the formal school curriculum. This is because the peculiar way in which outdoor education has developed (see for example Quay and Seaman, 2013) has resulted in an emphasis being placed on experience rather than on knowledge per se. The educational philosophy of John Dewey has played a significant part in assisting outdoor educators to understand and express their practice in theoretical terms, chiefly because of the 'intimate and necessary relation' he perceived 'between the processes of actual experience and education' (1938, 20).

Dewey's 'coherent theory of experience' (1938, 30) presents interpretative challenges, as acknowledged by many, including Richard Peters, whose supportive but also critical account of Dewey's philosophy of education has helped me to illuminate aspects of Dewey's theory of experience and its connection with education. My account of Dewey's philosophy, as presented here, has sought to acknowledge two significant conceptual elements that Peters either did not address, or addressed only minimally. Without awareness of Dewey's understanding of aesthetic experience, it is impossible to discern the coherence in his theory of experience. For Dewey philosophical work was not pragmatic alone. Similarly, without a deeper understanding of his sense of occupation, expressed in my words as being–doing–knowing, the finer details of this coherence can be overlooked, realising legitimate concerns.

Outdoor educators continue to explore theories of experience with the aim of better understanding their practice. Dewey's work makes an important contribution to that endeavour. It is my hope that mainstream educators can learn to better understand his theory of experience and education, resulting in a shift in the conceptualisation of both from knowing–doing–being, to being–doing–knowing.

References

Dewey, J. (1900). *The school and society*. Chicago: The University of Chicago Press (revised edition 1915).

Dewey, J. (1902). *The child and the curriculum*. Chicago: The University of Chicago Press.

Dewey, J. (1910). The influence of Darwinism on philosophy. In J. Dewey, *The influence of Darwin on philosophy and other essays in contemporary thought* (pp. 1–19). Bloomington: Indiana University Press.

Dewey, J. (1913). *Interest and effort in education*. Cambridge, MA: The Riverside Press.

Dewey, J. (1916a). *Democracy and education*. New York: The Free Press.

Dewey, J. (1916b). *Essays in experimental logic*. New York: Dover Publications.

Dewey, J. (1929). *The sources of a science of education*. New York: Liveright.

Dewey, J. (1930). From absolutism to experimentalism. In G. P. Adams and W. P. Montague (eds), *Contemporary American philosophy: Personal statements, Vol. 2* (pp. 13–27). New York: Russell and Russell.

Dewey, J. (1933). *How we think: A restatement of the relation of reflective thinking to the educative process* (rev. edn). Boston: D. C. Heath and Company.

Dewey, J. (1934). *Art as experience*. New York: Capricorn Books.

Dewey, J. (1935). The founder of pragmatism. *New Republic, 81*(30 January), 338–339.

Dewey, J. (1938). *Experience and education*. New York: Collier Books.

Dewey, J. (1939). Experience, knowledge and value: A rejoinder. In P. A. Schilpp (ed.), *The philosophy of John Dewey* (pp. 515–608). Evanston, IL: Northwestern University Press.

Dewey, J. (1940). Nature in experience. *Philosophical Review, 49*(2), 244–258.

Dewey, J. (1948). A comment on the foregoing criticisms. *The Journal of Aaesthetics and Art Criticism, 6*(3), 207–209.

Fallace, T. (2012). Recapitulation theory and the new education: Race, culture, imperialism, and pedagogy, 1894–1916. *Curriculum Inquiry, 42*(4), 510–533.

Martin, P. (2010). Outdoor education and the national curriculum in Australia. *Australian Journal of Outdoor Education, 14*(2), 3–11.

Ord, J. and Leather, M. (2011). The substance beneath the labels of experiential learning: The importance of John Dewey for outdoor educators. *Australian Journal of Outdoor Education, 15*(2), 13–23.

Pascucci, M. (2016). Deweyan aaesthetics as experiential education. *Journal of Philosophy and History of Education, 66*(1), 1–11.

Peters, R. S. (1965). Education as initiation. In R. D. Archambault (ed.), *Philosophical analysis and education* (pp. 87–111). New York: Humanities Press.

Peters, R. S. (1970a). Education and the educated man: Some further reflections. *Journal of Philosophy of Education, 4*(1), 5–20.

Peters, R. S. (1970b). *Ethics and education* (2nd edn). London: George Allen and Unwin.

Peters, R. S. (1973). *The philosophy of education*. London: Oxford University Press.

Peters, R. S. (1977). *Education and the education of teachers*. London: Routledge & Kegan Paul.

Pring, R. (2007). *John Dewey: A philosopher of education for our time?* London: Continuum

Quay, J. (2013). *Education, experience and existence: Engaging Dewey, Peirce and Heidegger*. Abingdon: Routledge.

Quay, J. (2015). *Understanding life in school: From academic classroom to outdoor education*. New York: Palgrave Macmillan.

Quay, J. and Seaman, J. (2013). *John Dewey and education outdoors: Making sense of the 'educational situation' through more than a century of progressive reforms*. Rotterdam, NL: Sense Publishers.

Seaman, J. (2008). Experience, reflect, critique: The end of the learning cycles era. *Journal of Experiential Education, 31*(1), 3–18.

Seaman, J., Brown, M. and Quay, J. (2017). The evolution of experiential learning theory: Tracing lines of research in the JEE. *Journal of Experiential Education, 40*(4), NP1–NP21.

Shulman, L. (1986). Those who understand: Knowledge growth in teaching. *Educational Researcher, 15*(2), 4–14.

Thorburn, M. (2018). Moral deliberation and environmental awareness: Reviewing Deweyan-informed possibilities for contemporary outdoor learning. *Journal of Adventure Education and Outdoor Learning, 18*(1), 26–35.

Thorburn, M. and Allison, P. (2017). Learning outdoors and living well? Conceptual prospects for enhancing curriculum planning and pedagogical practices. *Cambridge Journal of Education, 47*(1), 103–115.

7 The long-term influence of expeditions on people's lives

Maria-Jose Ramirez, Pete Allison,
Tim Stott and Aaron Marshall

Introduction

Adventure education programmes often aim to facilitate both personal and interpersonal growth (Martin, Cashel, Wagstaff and Breunig, 2006; Mutz and Müller, 2016) through, for example, youth expeditions, mountain centres, survival and wilderness courses among others (Allison, Stott, Felter and Beames, 2011). However, the underlying characteristics of adventure education programmes 'involve doing physically active things away from the person's normal environment' (Hattie, Marsh, Neill and Richards, 1997). According to Hattie *et al.* (1997) adventure programmes share six characteristics. They usually involve:

1 a small group of people;
2 pursuing mentally and/or physically challenging goals (e.g. hiking a peak, canoeing a river);
3 in a wilderness setting;
4 usually for 2 to 4 weeks duration;
5 usually involving group decision-making and problem-solving among participants;
6 with a non-intrusive, trained leader.

These programmes have reported a multitude of outcomes, such as improved self-concept, attitude, communication, leadership and teamwork (Chang, 2017; Deane and Harré, 2014; Hattie *et al.*, 1997) and these have been summarised by Mutz and Müller (2016, 106) as,

> a more positive self-concept and increased self-esteem (e.g. Belanger, McGowan, Lang, Bradley, & Courneya, 2013; Boeger, Dorfler, & Schut-Ansteeg, 2006; Epstein, 2004; Fengler & Schwarzer, 2008; Gehris, Kress, & Swalm, 2010; Gillespie & Allen-Craig, 2009; Probst

& Koesler, 1998; Schell, Cotton, & Luxmoore, 2012), improved cognitive autonomy (Margalit & Ben-Ari, 2014), reduced school truancy (Ang et al., 2014), more prosocial behaviour (Cook, 2008), the approval of nature protection (Martin, 2004; Palmberg & Kuru, 2000), increased group cohesion (Cooley, Burns, & Cumming, 2015; Greffrath, Meyer, Strydom, & Ellis, 2013), prejudice reduction (Wright & Tolan, 2009) and abstinence in regard to substance use (Carter, Straits, & Hall, 2007; Lewis, 2013). Reviews and meta-analyses show that the majority of studies have mostly concentrated on self-concept and group dynamics.

(Ewert and McAvoy, 2000; Gillis and Speelman, 2008; Hattie *et al.*, 1997; Stott, Allison, Felter and Beames, 2015)

Examining possible outcomes of outdoor experiential learning and adventure education programmes, Hattie *et al.* (1997) noted the wide variety of programmes offered, as well as the spread of the outcomes. They found 40 categories of outcomes, which they classified into six dimensions: leadership, self-concept, academic, personality, interpersonal and adventuresome. Independence, confidence, self-efficacy, self-understanding, assertiveness, internal locus of control and decision-making were the most significant outcomes observed, with self-control being the common underlying theme among them. They concluded that adventure programmes are positive experiences and provide a wide variety of outcomes ranging from academic performance to resilience, confidence and physical skills. They suggested that the influence of expeditions increases over time. However, the follow-up period was on average 5.5 months after the experience, which is not genuinely 'long-term' (as discussed below).

More recently, Stott *et al.* (2015) conducted a literature review and thematic analysis of research on youth expeditions post-2000. They organised their finding around Greenaway's (1995) four-arrows model of personal development (adapted from Giges and Rosenfeld, 1976), proposing that personal development through expeditions can be understood as growth in arrows pointing in four directions: upward, outward, inward and downward.

The upward arrow refers to realising potential and research has identified these outcomes as: more willingness to take challenges (Beames, 2005), enthusiasm (Stott and Hall, 2003), mental resilience (Beames, 2005), resilience (Ewert and Yoshino, 2011), ability to live in crowded circumstances (Stott and Hall, 2003), self-reliance (Ewert and Yoshino, 2011), confidence and self-reliance (Ashby, 1999).

The inward arrow is about learning about oneself, answering questions such as: Who am I? What I want/need/think? Some of the research outcomes placed in this category are, personal-emotional adjustment (Bobilya, Akey and Mitchell, 2009), increased ability to control emotions (Stott and Hall, 2003), reflection on values, self, life, career, friendships and relationships (Allison and Von Wald, 2010; Andrews, 1999), and spiritual development (Bobilya *et al.*, 2009).

The outward arrow refers to encountering and learning about others. Since expeditions involve working in groups, participants would usually develop social and collaborative skills, such as a sense of community (Andrews, 1999), interpersonal skills (Beames, 2005), and social adjustment (Bobilya *et al.*, 2009).

The downward arrow involves being grounded and connected, being more aware of the environment and appreciating it, and the degree to which participants feel connected to something greater than themselves. Outcomes include environmental appreciation (Allison, 1998, 2000, 2005), sense of place (Andrews, 1999) and global awareness (Sheldon, 2009).

Testimonials from alumni of youth outdoor adventure programmes such as Outward Bound, Class Afloat and the British Exploring Society, found in their respective websites, frequently refer to the expedition experience as a 'life-changing' one – where participants had the opportunity to know themselves better, gain skills and meet other people.

> The 6 months I spent at sea as a midshipman with Class Afloat in 1990 has left a lasting mark on my life, both personally and professionally. Life at sea taught me patience, teamwork, and persistence in a way that I have not seen matched in my 25-year career as a leader and educator. Equally important, experiencing other cultures on four continents provided me with a depth of understanding and enriched worldview that has benefitted me time and time again throughout my life.
>
> (Class Afloat alumnus (Class Afloat, n.d.))

> The expedition has been a life-changing adventure that I definitely didn't expect, with some incredible memories and some amazing people that won't ever be forgotten....
>
> (British Exploring Society alumni (British Exploring Society, n.d.))

> The greatest experience of my life where I was able to find myself and appreciate who I am and what I can offer the world.
>
> (Outward Bound alumni (Outward Bound, n.d.))

Despite the often-repeated rhetoric that expeditions are life-changing experiences, evidence on their long-term impact is scarce (Daniel, 2007;

Takano, 2010). Numerous studies have noted the need to observe the benefits attributed to expedition participation over extended periods of time
(e.g. Daniel, 2007; Stott *et al.*, 2015; Takano, 2010), but most empirical
studies typically examine the post-expedition experience six months to (at
most) five years afterwards, with Takano's (2010) study looking back over
20 years as an exception. Adventure education organisations have a
genuine need to conduct research, not only to inform future practices but
also to provide empirical evidence to back up their claims that the lessons
and skills acquired during youth expeditions are transferred into other life
contexts over an extended period – i.e. throughout life.

Purpose

We have been working on the long-lasting influence of expeditions over
the last ten years, which is an area that has received limited attention
despite its importance for the underpinning assumptions and assertions
often articulated the literature. In this chapter, we will give an overview of
three studies, focusing on the results. For the details of each of these
studies, please refer directly to them. These three studies relate to the
broader context of this book, examining different perspectives on concep-
tualising and understanding experiences outdoors.

Study 1: sailing to the virtues

Marshall *et al.* (in review) researched the perceptions of former participants of Class Afloat – a sailing voyage of one or two semesters involving
high school students, who also gained education credits for taking part.
Class Afloat, founded in 1984, is a residential tall ship sailing programme
that works with non-intact groups. Participants can join for a semester or a
year. Participants engage in a variety of international outdoor adventure
experiences combined with formal learning and community service. The
study focused on how the experience may have contributed to shaping
participants' identity, values and virtues.

Methods used were a survey and narrative interviews with former Class
Afloat participants with 1–27 years of retrospection. First, former participants received an electronic questionnaire inviting them to self-report their
programme experience and life story: 124 alumni responded. Then to
understand better and to gain insight regarding the variety of answers collected in the survey, 16 participants were approached for interview, reflect-
ing the diversity observed in the survey (gender, opinions, year of
participation). Interviews were analysed following phenomenological
approaches by theming the data with inductive and deductive themes.

Using an Aristotelian virtue lens to understand the personal and social development of participants during the expedition experience, Marshall *et al*. (in review) argued that character building develops over a lifetime and, as Aristotle suggests, the cultivation of practical wisdom can only be measured over a lifetime. Marshall *et al*. argued that Aristotle's approach is useful to understand better a long-term retrospective study. Four main themes emerged from the data: Significance, Practice, Values clarification and Friendships and Community.

First, Class Afloat alumni considered their experience as a significant one in their lives in comparison with other life experiences. In the survey, 96 per cent reported that the experience made a change in them, and when choosing three words to describe the experience 99 per cent of the words had a positive connotation and 40 per cent mentioned the phrase 'life-changing' or similar. The interviews reflected these results. Participants mentioned the significance or uniqueness of the experience and provided examples of its significance to their lives. The expedition influenced vocational choices, opened participants' eyes to understand future experiences, and provided a new paradigm for travelling, giving a global perspective and engagement with others. The expedition also provided a context in which participants could understand themselves and the world.

Second, most alumni reported the relevance of onboard chores, such as night watches, cleaning and cooking, to their experience. These duties fostered the development of habits/skills such as personal accountability, shared goals, community and reflective virtues. More interestingly, alumni reported using these learned habits and skills in later life and other life settings.

Third, the experience also facilitated values clarification, which also influenced life after the voyage. The different challenges experienced in Class Afloat helped participants to develop self-awareness, self-knowledge, self-identity and to think not only about themselves in a new way but also to practice what they have discovered about themselves in their life after the trip.

Finally, the voyage facilitated friendships and community building. The fact that Class Afloat was a non-intact group, where participants did not know each other before the voyage, as well as living in close proximity with others for a set amount of time, with a shared goal, facilitated the development of new friendships and community building.

Marshall *et al*. (in revision) conclude that Class Afloat participants perceive their experience as significant in their personal and social development not only in the voyage but the life after it, influencing their concept of personal identity, their later careers, marriage and parenthood. This indicates that some of this learning takes some time to be processed.

Study 2: mountaineering and canoeing

Allison *et al.* (in review) researched the long-term outcomes of three canoe and mountaineering high school expeditions organised by the staff and students of a Scottish high school in the 1970s. The expeditions were 1-month long, with intact groups who went to France, Switzerland, Spain and Austria. The experience also included a year-long preparation phase leading to the expedition, in which teachers and students built canoes and trained and competed in canoeing or hill walking. More specifically, this study examined participants' memories of their motivation to get involved in the experience and the perceived retrospective personal benefits of participating (personal and social development) 40 years after the experience.

In common with Marshall *et al.* the research design comprised two phases. The first entailed 45 life stories completed by participants over the internet. Six general themes were provided as prompts: *Short life story*; *Key life moments*; *Interesting events*; *Funny events*; *CV relevant content*; and *Lasting memory from their expedition.* All stories were read, and the researchers extracted the data and organised it into a Microsoft Excel summary table, which helped researchers to familiarise themselves with the participants.

The second phase comprised ten individual face-to-face interviews with participants who were selected from the life stories. The interviewees were five males and five females aged 53 to 55, who had been students on one or more of the expeditions. The interviews lasted approximately 30 minutes and took place during a reunion organised by the Principal Teacher of Physical Education at the school who organised the expeditions. The purpose of the interviews was to gain an understanding of what participants perceived they learned or gained from the expedition experience. A schedule for the semi-structured interviews was developed based on reviewed literature and themes identified within the first phase document analysis. All interviews were recorded and transcribed, in order to perform a thematic analysis.

The Allison *et al.* study concluded that the expedition had a long-lasting influence on participants even 40 years after the experience in their personal and professional lives. They identified five main themes from the thematic analysis.

First, the experience helped students to develop their *confidence and independence.* The challenges overcome on the trip helped participants to have a similar attitude in life, to push their boundaries, and be open to challenges even when being afraid. A second lasting lesson from the trip was the *planning and preparation.* Since the beginning, students were involved in planning the trip. There was extensive preparation that involved building canoes and physical training, as well as planning the destinations and campsite arrangements that had to be done by postal mail since at that time (1970s) the internet was not available. A third aspect identified was the *teamwork/group bonding/friendships* developed during the trip. Tasks and responsibilities were divided among the strengths and skills of each participant that facilitated their sense of belonging in the group. Students also reported learning about *optimism, effort and perseverance*. Participants noted their willingness to work hard and the effort they dedicated to this expedition in order for it to succeed. Several participants reported that the effort and perseverance was something they carried on into their lives after the trip. Finally, particip-ants noted that trips such as the one in which they participated are not fre-quent these days. They recognised the extra effort that their teachers dedicated to it and the number of regulatory permits which would be necessary nowadays, which made them feel *gratitude and the desire to offer service* – they were grateful for the experience, which helped them to realise the relevance of giving back to the community in different ways (teaching, volunteering, mentoring and service in the schools of their own children).

Study 3: science and adventure

Ramirez (in preparation) researched the perceived long-lasting influence of a British Exploring Society expedition. The British Exploring Society is a UK-based youth charity, founded in 1932 by Surgeon Commander George Murray Levick. Since its formation, the society has continued to grow, organising 3–6-week-long land-based self-sufficient expeditions for non-intact groups, to conduct research in a variety of climates and remote locations for young people aged between 16 and 25 years.

Drawing on methods developed by Marshall *et al.* (in review) this third study also used a retrospective approach and had two phases: first, an online survey was sent to all the British Exploring Society members, fol-lowed by individual interviews in a second phase. The purpose of the survey was to identify emerging themes surrounding the influence of the expedition experience in the explorers' lives, and to identify potential interviewees for the second phase. The survey was answered by 158 people with 5–70 years of retrospection. In the second phase, 26 semi-structured individual interviews were conducted with former young explorers of expeditions that took place 29–60 years ago. The interviews addressed how the experience might have influenced participants' lives, beliefs, and choices. All interviews were recorded and transcribed, in order to perform a thematic analysis.

Table 7.1 Summary of methods of the three studies

Study	Activity	Duration	Methods	Retrospection	Type of group
Sailing	Tall ship Community service	1 semester 1 year	Survey 124 Interviews 16	1–27	Non-intact group
Mountaineering and canoeing	Canoe and trekking	1 month	Life-story 45 Interviews 12	40 years	Intact group
Science and adventure	Trekking and science projects	5 weeks	Survey 103 Interviews 18+	30–50 years	Non-intact group

Ramirez (in preparation) concluded that, in general, the expedition was a positive experience for participants. The degree of influence of the expedition varied. For some, it had a generally positive influence even if they had a difficult time articulating the type of influence; while for others the expedition experience was seen as a stepping-stone or a reinforcement of previous choices; and for yet others it was a life-changing experience. Participants perceived mainly six types of long-lasting influence from the expedition.

First, participants reported that the expedition helped them to *increase their confidence and achieve their potential*, by developing their physical and social resilience and their ability to overcome challenges and persevere in difficult situations. Second, the expedition provided opportunities for reflection and to learn from difficult experiences. This allowed participants to *learn more about themselves*, to reflect on their values, self, life, career, friendships and relationships, gaining a greater understanding of themselves that they had not known before. Self-discovery was a significant life impact that was being carried for the rest of the explorer's life. Third, participants also noted how the experience helped them to *learn about and relate to others*, to develop social skills by experiencing the challenges of interpersonal relationships.

The fourth long-lasting influence of the expedition was the *transfer to others*. The knowledge and the skills learned in the expedition were later transferred to others such as participants' families, friends, children and grandchildren as well as to others with whom participants volunteered or taught. Participants also perceived the expedition as having a significant life impact on their outdoor knowledge and skills. They refer to their *increased outdoor skills* as having the feeling that they can go anywhere and to organise an expedition by themselves, which also *influenced their leisure choices*, such as travel destinations or to continue camping (or not to). Finally, some participants reported a perceived change in participants' appreciation for the environment, nature and the outdoors since the expedition increased their *environmental awareness and appreciation*.

Discussion

The three retrospective studies presented explored the perceived long-lasting influence of expedition in participants' lives. The settings for each study differ, Marshall *et al.* (in review) studied a six and 12 month sailing programme, Allison *et al.* (in review) explored a month-long canoe and trekking high school expedition while Ramirez (in preparation) focused on 3–6-week adventure and science expeditions to remote places. Marshall *et al.* and Ramirez studied non-intact groups that got together for the

Table 7.2 Summary of results of the three studies

4 arrows	Sailing	Mountaineering and canoeing	Science and adventure
	Significance:	—	*Degree of influence of the expedition*
	96% reported that the experience made a change in them.		Degree in which the expedition influenced participants' life: From being challenging to articulate the influence of the expedition, to confirm and reinforce previous preferences to being a 'life changing' experience.
	40% mentioned the phrase 'life-changing' or a similar one.		
	Types of significance:		
	• Vocational choices • Eye opening to understand future experiences. New paradigm for travelling, gave a global perspective and engaging with others • Provided with a context to understand themselves and the world		

Upward arrow Realizing potential	Practice:	Confidence and independence:	Confidence and achieving one's potential:
	Relevance of onboard chores, such as night watches, cleaning and cooking, to their experience. Ship duties fostered the development of habits/skills such as: • Confidence • Optimism • Personal accountability • Shared goals • Community • Reflective virtues • Regulation by others Alumni reported using these learned aspects in later life and in other life settings.	Expedition experience gave confidence and bravery to do other challenging things later in life, even when fear was present. The expedition allowed them to be open to challenges, push boundaries while having fun.	Participants reported that the expedition helped them to increase their confidence and achieve their potential, by developing physical and social resilience and their ability to overcome challenges and persevere in difficult situations.

continued

Table 7.2 Continued

4 arrows	Sailing	Mountaineering and canoeing	Science and adventure
Inward arrow	Values clarification:	Optimism, effort and perseverance:	Learning about oneself:
Learning about oneself	Challenges experienced help participants to: • Push participants to new limits and break through • Accelerate personal growth/growing up • Develop self-awareness • Develop self-knowledge • Develop self-identity • Think about themselves in a new way • Think differently about the world • Broadened global perspective • Practice what they have discovered about themselves in their life after the trip.	Learning of an attitude associated with optimism, effort and perseverance that took different forms depending on the individual. Attribution of a willingness to work hard and put in the effort to succeed and that this effort create an optimism that it is possible to achieve dreams/make aspirations into reality. Individuals reported this happening in other aspects of their lives including work, family and recreation activities.	The expedition provided opportunities for reflection and to learn from difficult experiences facilitating participants to learn more about themselves, to reflect on their values, self, life, career, friendships and relationships, gaining a greater understanding of themselves that they had not known before. Self-discovery as a significant life impact being carried with for the rest of the explorer's life.

Outward arrow	Friendships and community:	Teamwork/group bonding/ friendships:	Learning about and relating to others:
Encountering and learning about others	Conditions:	Every person in the group had a place. During the expedition everyone had a task and responsibilities in the group related to the students' strengths. They had a strong sense of independence by being away for a month and having to speak another language.	Participants also noted how the experience helped them to learn about and relate to others, to develop social skills by experiencing the challenges of inter-personal relationships.
	• Isolation from former communities		
	• Proximity with new people		
	• Time		
	• Shared goals and obligations on board.		
		None of the participants interviewed had stayed in touch with each other of other expedition members unless they had met before the expedition. However, many reported that they can pick up where they left off no problem. Stories, 'banter' and culture all come back, they did not feel that 40 years had passed.	

continued

Table 7.2 Continued

4 arrows	Sailing	Mountaineering and canoeing	Science and adventure
Outward arrow modified	—	*Gratefulness and service:*	*Transfer to others:*
		Several participants commented that currently kids do not have the opportunity to undertake trips like this.	The knowledge and the skills learned in the expedition is later transferred to others such as participants' families, friends, children, and grandchildren as well as to others with whom participants volunteered, or taught.
		Several participants believed in the importance of helping the next generation. They found different ways of volunteering and giving back to community through teaching, volunteering, mentoring, other forms of service or being involved in their own children's school planning.	
	—	Planning and preparation: Prior to the expedition there was extensive preparation (building canoes, training). There was also extensive planning regarding the campsites and where they were going to go.	—

Increased outdoor knowledge/skills:

| Explorers perceived the expedition as having a significant life impact on their outdoor knowledge and skills. They refer to their increased outdoor skills as having the feeling that they can go anywhere and to organize an expedition by themselves, which also influenced their leisure choices, such as travel destinations or to continue camping (or not to).

Learning about environment:

Degree to which the expedition facilitated a change in participants' appreciation for the environment, nature and the outdoors since the expedition increased their environmental awareness and appreciation.

Downward arrow

Being grounded and connected

expedition, while Allison *et al.* observed intact groups in a high school that planned and prepared for one year.

The three studies concluded that, in general, the expedition experience was positive for participants, but in different degrees of significance. For some, it was just a good experience, while for others it was a stepping-stone or an experience that helped them to mature faster, and still for others a life-changing one. The three studies reported participants saying the phrase that the experience was 'life-changing', which speaks to the prevailing rhetoric of these experiences. However, more important than identifying and debating whether or not expeditions are or not life-changing experiences, is to understand in which ways these experiences influence people's lives, since this can inform future programmes and youth development organisations.

In the literature review and thematic analysis conducted by Stott *et al.* (2015), the primary outcomes of adventure education programmes were organised according to the four-arrows model of personal development (Greenaway, 1995). Even if each study differs in the names of the themes identified, the results of the three studies presented in this chapter coincide with three of the arrows, upward (realising potential), inward (learning about oneself) and outward (encountering and learning about others).

Marshall *et al.* (in review) argue that the *practice*, the onboard chores on the ship, fostered the development of habits and skills such as confidence, perseverance, optimism, and personal accountability. Similarly, Allison *et al.* (in review) reported that students had developed confidence and independence to do other challenging things in life, while Ramirez (in preparation) noted how participants perceived that the expedition fostered their confidence and achieved their potential by overcoming physical and mental challenges, something that they have carried with them. These three themes coincide with the upward arrow of personal development (Greenaway, 1995).

A second outcome that participants reported in the three studies was that the expedition experience provided a space to learn about themselves. Marshal *et al.* (in review) mentioned how the challenges experienced helped participants to clarify their values and learn more about themselves. In the same way, Ramirez (in preparation) noted that the expedition provided opportunities for reflection and to learn from difficult experiences facilitating participants to learn more about themselves, to reflect on their values, self, life, career, friendships and relationships, gaining a greater understanding of themselves than they had before. Allison *et al.* (in review) identified that the students developed an attitude of optimism, effort and perseverance. These outcomes align with the inward arrow of personal development (Greenaway, 1995).

The third common theme was the development of friendships and community (Marshall *et al.*, in review), teamwork/group bonding/friendships (Allison *et al.*, in review) and learning about and relating to others (Ramirez, in preparation), which reflects the outward arrow of personal development (Greenaway, 1995). Marshall *et al.* argue that the isolation from former communities, the interactions with new people, the time and the shared goals and obligations on board are the conditions that foster friendship and community – conditions that are present in the three studies.

The three common outcomes of the three studies, the increased confidence, learning about oneself and learning about others, coincide with the developmental tasks of the life period in which the expeditions took place. Expeditions are rich environments where people encounter new situations, face new challenges and meet new people in the wilderness (Allison and Von Wald, 2010; Shellman, 2014; Takano, 2010), providing many opportunities for young people to explore in an intense period. Expeditions usually take place during the adolescence and emerging adulthood years, which are vital stages for identity development. In fact, during adolescence, many biological, physical and cognitive changes are experienced (Arnett, 2007). In this stage, adolescents' greater cognitive capacity allows them to think scientifically, to reflect, reason about abstract concepts (such as friendship, loyalty, freedom), consider different perspectives and perceive different aspects of a situation (complex thinking), examine their thoughts and thought processes (metacognition), and see themselves in a third person – abilities that children lack and all of which provide fertile ground for identity development (Arnett, 2007; Woolfolk, 2010). Roeser and Pinela (2014) argue that adolescence provides a window of opportunity for communities to have a positive influence on adolescents since they are typically more open and have a desire to become contributing members of society. The emerging adulthood years are years of exploration, since most people make life choices at that time that have lasting effects, such as marriage and career choices (Arnett, 2007). Therefore, the long-term influences found in the three studies, regarding confidence, learning about oneself and learning about others, reflect the developmental tasks of these life stages and the opportunity that experiences like expeditions provide for young people to explore and prepare them to take the decisions that will have lasting effects.

The studies differ in four areas. For instance, only Ramirez (in preparation) reported that the expedition increased participants' environmental awareness and appreciation for the environment, nature and the outdoors, corresponding to the downward arrow of personal development. A related theme that was also particular to the Ramirez study was the increased outdoor knowledge/skills. Participants referred to their increased outdoor skills and the feeling that they could go anywhere and could organise an expedition by themselves, which in turn influenced their leisure choices, such as travel destinations or to continue camping (or not to). The different settings in which the expeditions took place can explain these aspects. The expeditions of the British Exploring Society are characterised by remoteness and self-sufficiency. Participants go to remote areas for three to six weeks, something that did not occur in the high school expedition or Class Afloat, since they went to more urban settings and they were not self-sufficient.

An outcome that was present in two of the three studies (Allinson and Ramirez) is the theme of gratefulness and service, as well as the transfer to others (in Ramirez). Participants in both of these studies reflected on how fortunate they were to be able to participate in an expedition, how much they appreciated the leaders and how much they felt the importance of giving back what they received. This aspect can be an extension to the outward arrow (Greenaway, 1995), an outcome that may take many years to develop.

The last outcome that only emerged in the Allison study was planning and preparation. A particular characteristic of the high school canoe and trekking expeditions was that they each took a year of preparation. During this preparation, students built canoes and were in charge of organising the route and the lodging – something that did not happen in Class Afloat or the British Exploring Society, since these expeditions were managed by established organisations that took care of the logistics. So it is not surprising that only participants of the high school expeditions learned the importance of planning and preparation for the expedition.

Conclusions and implications for practice and research

Few studies are available from which we can assess the long-term outcomes of youth expeditions. Here, three retrospective studies that explored the perceived long-lasting influence of expeditions in participants' lives are reported and synthesised. The settings for each study differed. The three studies outlined in this chapter all identified three common outcomes of youth expeditions: increased confidence, learning about oneself and learning about others. Only the Ramirez study, which involved participants operating in remote or wilderness areas, reported that expeditions increased participants' environmental awareness and appreciation for the environment, nature and the outdoors. The other two studies did not take place in wilderness areas and arguably required less self-sufficiency. Two of the three studies identified the theme gratefulness and service (Allison *et al.*, in review) and the transfer to others in Ramirez (in preparation). Participants in both of these studies reflected on how fortunate they were to participate in an expedition, how much they appreciated the leaders and how much they noticed the importance of giving back what they received. The last outcome identified, planning and preparation, was only identified in the Allison *et al.* study. This was because these high school expeditions each took a year of preparation, which did not happen in Class Afloat or the British Exploring Society.

This chapter provides a synthesis of three currently unpublished studies that shed some further light on the long-term outcomes for participants of three different types of youth expeditions. In terms of implications for future practice, the key conclusion is that these studies confirm the importance and long-term value of such expeditions to young people and add vital evidence to the case for building such opportunities into young people's lives.

While we believe that these three studies begin to fill a gap in our knowledge and understanding about the longer-term impacts of expeditions, we feel that these studies just provide a starting point for what we see a very fruitful avenue for future research.

Bibliography

Allison, P. (1998). Greenland: More questions than answers. *Horizons, 2*, 16–20.

Allison, P. (2000). *Research from the ground up: Post expedition adjustment.* Cumbria: Brathay Hall Trust.

Allison, P. (2005). Post-expedition adjustment: What empirical data suggest. In *National Conference on Outdoor Leadership*, Estes Park, CO.

Allison, A. (in review). *40 years on: Just how 'life-changing' are school expeditions?*

Allison, P., Stott, T., Felter, J. and Beames, S. (2011). Overseas youth expeditions. In M. Berry and C. Hodgson (Eds), *Adventure education* (pp. 187–205). New York, NY: Routledge.

Allison, P. and Von Wald, K. (2010). Exploring values and personal and social development: Learning through expeditions. *Pastoral Care in Education, 28*(3), 219–233.

Andrews, K. (1999). The wilderness expedition as a rite of passage: Meaning and process in experiential education. *Journal of Experiential Education, 22*(1), 35–43.

Arnett, J. J. (2007). *Adolescence and emerging adulthood: A cultural approach* (3rd ed.). Upper Saddle River, NJ: Pearson Prentice Hall.

Ashby, M. (1999). The educational role of expeditions. *Teaching Geography, 24*(3), 122–125.

Beames, S. (2005). Expeditions and the social construction of the self. *Australian Journal of Outdoor Education, 9*(1), 14–22.

Bobilya, A. J., Akey, L. and Mitchell, D., Jr. (2009). Outcomes of a spiritually focussed wilderness orientation programme. *Journal of Experiential Education, 33*(4), 440–443.

British Exploring Society (n.d.). Testimonials. Retrieved 10 January 2010, from www.britishexploring.org/join-an-expedition/testimonials.aspx.

Chang, Y. (2017). *Exploring the effect of autonomous student experiences on positive youth development* (Doctoral dissertation thesis). Indiana University.

Class Afloat (n.d.). Our alumni. Retrieved 10 January 2010, from www.classafloat.com/our-alumni/.

Daniel, B. (2007). The life significance of a spiritually oriented, Outward Bound-type wilderness expedition. *Journal of Experiential Education, 29*(3), 386–389.

Deane, K. L. and Harré, N. (2014). The youth adventure programming model. *Journal of Research on Adolescence, 24*(2), 293–308.

Ewert, A. and McAvoy, L. (2000). *The effects of wilderness settings on organized groups: A state-of-knowledge paper*. Proceedings RMRS-P-15-VOL-3. Wilderness science in a time of change conference, Missoula, MT Vol. 3, pp. 13–26. Ogden, UT: US Department of Agriculture, Forest Service, Rocky Mountain Research Station (Vol. 3, pp. 13–26).

Ewert, A. and Yoshino, A. (2011). The influence of short-term adventure-based experiences on levels of resilience. *Journal of Adventure Education and Outdoor Learning, 11*(1), 35–50.

Giges, B. and Rosenfeld, E. (1976). Personal growth, encounter and self-awareness groups. In M. Rosenbaum and A. Snadowsky (Eds), *The intensive group experience*. New York, NY: Free Press.

Gillis, L. H. and Speelman, E. (2008). Are challenge (ropes) courses an effective tool? A meta-analysis. *Journal of Experiential Education, 31*(2), 111–135.

Greenaway, R. (1995). In search of respectable adventure. *Horizons, 14*(4), 24–26.

Hattie, J., Marsh, H. W., Neill, J. T. and Richards, G. E. (1997). Adventure education and Outward Bound: Out-of-class experiences that make a lasting difference. *Review of Educational Research, 67*(1), 43–87.

Marshall, A. (2016). *Toward understanding perceived growth in practical wisdom*. Edinburgh: The University of Edinburgh.

Marshall, A., Allison, P. and Hearn, J. (in review). *The question of significance.*

Martin, B., Cashel, C., Wagstaff, M. and Breunig, M. (2006) *Outdoor leadership: Theory and practice*. Champaign, IL: Human Kinetics.

Mutz, M. and Müller, J. (2016). Mental health benefits of outdoor adventures: Results from two pilot studies. *Journal of Adolescence, 49*, 105–114.

Outward Bound (n.d.). What our students say. Retrieved 10 January 2010, from www.outwardbound.org/classic/adventure-trips-testimonials/.

Ramirez, M. J. (in preparation). What is the perceived long-term influence of expedition 30 years after?

Roeser, R. W. and Pinela, C. (2014). Mindfulness and compassion training in adolescence: a developmental contemplative science perspective. *New Directions for Youth Development*, (142), 9–30.

Sheldon, R. (2009). *Rallying together: A research study of Raleigh's work with disadvantaged young people*. London: Institute for Public Policy Research.

Shellman, A. (2014). Empowerment and experiential education: A state of knowledge paper. *Journal of Experiential Education, 37*(1), 18–30.

Stott, T., Allison, P., Felter, J. and Beames, S. (2015). Personal development on youth expeditions: a literature review and thematic analysis. *Leisure Studies, 34*(2), 197–229.

Stott, T. A. and Hall, N. E. (2003). Changes in aspects of students' self-reported personal, social and technical skills during a six-week wilderness expedition in Arctic Greenland. *Journal of Adventure Education and Outdoor Learning, 3*(2), 159–169.

Takano, T. (2010). A 20-year retrospective study of the impact of expeditions on Japanese participants. *Journal of Adventure Education and Outdoor Learning, 10*(2), 77–94.

Woolfolk, A. (2010). *Psicología Educativa*. Mexico: Pearson Education.

8 Transformative experience as a change of horizon

Ivo Jirásek

Difficulties in the theoretical understanding of experience

One of the main issues at the forefront of the interest of the constituent theoretical field of experiential pedagogy that reflects the educational tendency of holistic (outdoor, adventure and experiential) education is a philosophical model that points to the transformational potential of a physically anchored experience. Specifically, how can even a short-term intervention in the form of an experiential course cause the whole of a human life to be transformed from a long-term perspective? The phenomenon of experience and its transformative potential is becoming a key topic for deeper consideration.

Experience cannot be narrowed down only to rational discourse and a logical calculus; therefore, philosophical reflections on experience cannot be avoided without a psychological analysis of imagination, fantasy and intuition, without passion and spontaneity, feelings and strong emotions, and without human life in its full breadth, formed differently from mere intellectual opinion.

This is the deeper problem that faces contemporary Western science: many experiences whose relevance is not doubted by those who have them cannot be explained rationally in the paradigm of the 'normal sciences' (Kuhn, 1962), which is built on the assumption of the exclusively material form of the world in three-dimensional space and linear time. The usual scientific approach of Western civilization is seen as increasingly unhelpful in understanding experiences that cannot be attributed merely to sense illusions or mental illnesses. Near-death experiences, in which a person experiences moving beyond the boundaries of body-related consciousness (Moody, 1975), or when a blind individual from birth can perceive visual perceptions (Ring and Cooper, 1997) pose psychological and philosophical questions of great concern. Extraordinary states of consciousness, whether induced by psychedelics (Grof, 1972, 1977), holotropic breathing (Grof and Grof, 2010), or the perception of art (Zuska, 1994) problematise and question the usual understanding of time and space and the relationship between body and spirit.

It appears that it is insufficient to accept a science based exclusively on the analysis of matter, in order fully to understand human experience; it is also necessary to accept aspects of the spiritual world, the world behind sensory experience and the world of creative imagination and symbolic understanding. This is the imaginal world, *mundus imaginalis* (Corbin, 2007), which, unlike the world of the imaginary, fantasy, the unreal and mere visions or phantasmagoria, is a specific order of reality within the boundaries of being and existence. Linking the sphere of the spiritual world and the world of everyday living to holistic human experience can also be aided by experiential education, in which both types of experience evidently manifest (Haluza-Delay, 2000; Hitzhusen, 2004; Jirásek *et al.*, 2017; Stringer and McAvoy, 1992). Pedagogy should follow the path that humanistic and transpersonal psychology has already travelled, by being able to accept the spiritual dimension of reality as a necessary and integral part of the human psyche (Grof, 2003, 2008; Jaffé, 1989; Jung, 1964; Maslow, 1994, 2011).

An experience may undoubtedly have profound transformational potential, not necessarily solely due to the following reflections. Among the basic experiences of life is certainly the experience of love – a loving, caring relationship that philosophical tradition has identified as a desire for wholeness, beauty, and goodness (Plato, 1997) or love in different modes, such as erotic love, maternal love, love of one's home-land or love of God (Fromm, 1956). The experience of love is a force that 'moves mountains' and clearly changes the whole of one's life. Another experience that transforms the horizon of the meaning and purpose of life is a contact with death. The desire to overcome death is an archetypal element of culture, as evidenced by ancient Egyptian reli-gion, original Mesopotamian myths, or the Eleusinian mysteries (Bottéro, 2001, Eliade, 1981, Heller, 1988, Michalson, 2005, George, 2003). Death is the horizon of human life and an inseparable part of life, when our own life becomes being-unto-death (Heidegger, 2008). However, the transformation to the authentic mode of existence is also made possible by the full experience of the death of a close person, because this pro-foundly and substantially penetrates one's own existence (Landsberg, 1990). The experience of religious conversion (Augustine, 1966), a totally transforming, life-targeting value orientation, is the third prelimi-nary demonstration of a strenuous experience, which essentially shapes the overall transformation of life.

However, the aim of this text is not a detailed elaboration of individual experiential modes that we can perceive as the source of the transformation of life. Our basic point of view is experience framed by the possibilities of an experiential education programme, and a generalised reflection on its transformative power. We present religious and psychological terms concerning human experience in the mode of extraordinary states of consciousness (mystical experiences, peak experiences, flow, holotropic experiences, etc.) and their connection to the philosophical understanding of 'horizon', with the possibilities of its transformation. Thus, it is possible to describe a model of transformative experience that changes the life of an individual, which is fully applicable to the experience of holistic (outdoor, adventure and experiential) education and its analysis by experiential pedagogy.

An analysis of experience in religious science and psychology

Religious experiences

However, we are entering into a pedagogical reflection on the transformative power of experience with a certain detour through different disciplines, such as religion and psychology. The subject of experience has been richly developed in these discourses, and much of the acquired knowledge can subsequently be transposed into an educational dimension.

Religious experience is characterised by the widening or, more precisely, the 'othering' of the mode of consciousness that characterises the everydayness with the procurement of life needs and its practicalities. Entering into the sacred sphere of the 'absolutely other' is made possible by the attitude of celebration and participation in ritual, which is the answer to the facts of life and the understanding of existence as a gift (Sokol, 2004). Although the classic definition of sacred and profane (Eliade, 1959) considers the sacred and secular realms to be two existential ways of experiencing – the two modalities of being in the world – one can also consider the ontological differences of these two dimensions. The world of actual living is defined by normal states of consciousness characterised by rational and emotional control. The world of religion fundamentally differs in its basic characteristics, such as deity versus humanity, immortality versus mortality, infinity versus ultimate existence, and so on. What is essential for religion is therefore 'absolutely different' and 'absolutely other'. Additionally, it is possible to enter into this world exclusively through an experience that is constituted by an attitude of faith, which is radically different from a rational or volitional cognitive approach. The act of faith and belief essentially transforms the under-standing of the hierarchy of space and time and impregnates any human activity with the spiritual dimension (Eliade, 1971). Contact with the sacred for a religious person is a meeting with something hidden, unspeakable and *numinous*, and is accompanied by the mysterious tremor of *mysterium tremendum*, which is connected to the grandiose nobility of majesty, and to the attractive and the fascinating (Otto, 1958).

Religion often provides an illustration of a horizon's transformation through a one-time experiential impulse in the phenomenon of conversion. The change of religious consciousness, the adoption of a comprehensive system of a new interpretation of one's own life in the intention of faith, is a profound personal transformation and a life change. Accepted ideas, values, attitudes and social anchoring radically and totally change an individual's identity. Sudden dramatic conversion under the impression of a specific, time-limited and emotionally strong religious experience accompanied by temporary blindness is documented by Paul of Tarsus on his way to Damascus (the conversion of Saul, a persecutor of Christians, is discussed in the Acts of the Apostles, Chapter 9). However, a progressive intellectual examination and rational thinking about the consequences of conversion is shown, for example, in Augustine's memoirs (Augustine, 1966).

The religious experience of emotional movement and ecstasy has many different layers and is internally richly structured. There are different individual ascetic experiences of mental power and chastity or modesty; other experiences are the social experiences of love of one's nearest and dearest; and mercy, the most striking mystical experience, is difficult to communicate with words (James, 1985). Thus, the ecstatic states communicated by mystics cannot be described without symbols, metaphors, allegories and images from various areas of life, including the erotic, which is why the mysticism of Spain is called the mysticism of love. Mystical experiences are accompanied by rich visualisations and imagination, and many aspects of the events that are experienced represent mysteries for science that remain rationally unexplained (Třísková, 1997).

The example of religious experiences, which often influence the whole life through unique visions or mystical ecstasy, motivate us to ask whether a similarly radical change can be experienced in a non-religious context, even if these changes can be achieved through purposeful pedagogical action, including the possibilities and means of experiential education.

116   *Ivo Jirásek*

Peak experiences

We are particularly interested in an important meaning shift within pedagogical discourse that Abraham Maslow conducted in his study of religious experiences by using peak experiences (Maslow, 1962, 1994).
Maslow sees unusual connections and similarities between experiences
that are traditionally perceived as religious, mystical and spiritual and peak
experiences that even non-religious people in a state of full self-
actualisation achieve when they have fully developed their potential. Religious or mystical experiences and peak experiences are moments of great
astonishment, intense happiness or ecstatic exaltation and bliss, where
doubts, fears, tensions and weaknesses disappear. The same type of experimental response in the religious and mystical context is induced by other
situations, such as aesthetic, creative, love or sexual experiences, sports
and dance, listening to music, experiencing nature (especially in the
woods, in the mountains and at sea), moments of insight or discovery,
childbirth or cohabitation with other people. Thus, peak experiences are
transcendental and spiritual but are not exclusively religious; they are fully
found in the order of natural reality.

The world is perceived as a united, unified whole in a peak experience,
where one's attention is fully focused on perception, not evaluation, and
when an individual uses all of his or her capabilities to their full functionality. Human beings are filled with astonishment, humility and respect,
rather than their own self-interest. Experience exceeds ego and is perceived as a highly valuable and meaningful part of life. There is a disori-
entation in time and space and the perception of beauty and goodness,
while accepting evil as an essential part of the whole. The stimulus for a
peak experience can be a variety of activities, but it is not the most
important part of the activity, which is instead ecstatic, blissful perception
and the feeling of great happiness and fulfilment during the experience. At
the same time, peak experiences cannot be induced consciously; they
invade people unexpectedly. They cannot be targeted; they appear as a by-
product of full identification with an activity. However, what is most
important to us is that these experiences are transient, temporary, provi-
sional and not permanent, but their effects may be lasting. 'Sometimes
their after-effects are so profound and so great as to remind us of the profound religious conversions which forever after changed the person. Lesser
effects could be called therapeutic' (Maslow, 1994, p. 66).

The concept of peak experiences soon became a popular tool of empirical research, including its operationalisation (Thorne, 1963) and the use of
a conventional scale (Hallaq, 1977). The findings include, for example, the
knowledge that although girls are significantly more likely than boys to

feel the peak experience of being loved, boys are more likely to succeed, compete and win (Maslow, 1962). Male university students consider sexual sensuality to be the peak experience more often than women, but if sexuality is emotionally experienced in the context of love, it is acceptable to both groups (Allen *et al.*, 1964). Students gain most of their peak experiences during sports, artistic, religious or nature-based activities or through confidential moments with friends and family members (Polyson, 1985). The frequency of gaining peak experiences increases with age (Hallaq, 1977). Individuals with low adherence to conventional traditional religious beliefs feel more peak experiences than individuals with a high degree of religious belief (Breed and Fagan, 1972).

It is extremely important in the context of this publication that peak experiences often occur in a sporting environment – for example, when riding on mountain bikes (Dodson, 1996) – and show some differences in qualities, such as being more physically anchored and less cognitive or reflective in nature; or that a certain degree of attainment of basic skills is needed to achieve peak sporting experiences (Ravizza, 1977). A physical activity and the realisation of the programme in a natural environment are basic tools for experiential education. Nature supports the activation of peak experiences through its aesthetic qualities, because it is distanced from pressure, dispersion and the human world, and it possesses the possibility of individual spiritual expression (McDonald *et al.*, 2009).

Nadir experiences

It could be said that the experiences of the nadir are symmetrically opposite to peak experiences. Peak experiences are characterised by a high level of excitement or are perceived as the highest or the best experiences in life, whereas nadir experiences are perceived as the lowest, most marginal points of life or, in other words, the worst, most unpleasant and most distressing moments of life (Thorne, 1963). This does not mean, however, that nadir experiences do not affect individuals by changing the future of their lives.

Vivid experiences

If we combine the peak and nadir experiences, we find that their common denominations are lively, clear and intense: they are vivid experiences that represent the concept as somewhat broader and wider, emotionally neutral and more abstract. Ordinary populations tend to have more peak experiences than nadir experiences, while psychotic individuals do not show a significant difference between the two types of experiences (Margoshes and Litt, 1966).

Flow experiences

Another way of experiencing, that is full of positive dimensions and that is stimulated by various activities, is the flow experience, introduced by Mihalyi Csikszentmihalyi (1975a, 1975b). Flow is characterised by a full immersion in an activity, and it is notable that recreational activities such as rock climbing, chess, dance, basketball and music composition were analysed first. Such a full immersion brings joy on its own and is intrinsically satisfying or rewarding. Flow is therefore autotelic; no goals or external rewards are needed. Concentration becomes so important that time consciousness disappears; an experiencing person forgets his/her problems and his/her separate identity and gains full control over the action, without feeling anything other than activity itself. The level of skill fully corresponds to the complexity of the tasks, and the individual is therefore not even in the realm of worry or boredom, but just in flow.

The developmental nature of the concept of flow consists of increasing skills by the realisation of tasks and thus by requiring more challenging opportunities, so that the experience does not fall into the area of overly low challenges and the experience of boredom. Joyful experiences are characterised by moving forward, the feeling of novelty and the achievement of a goal. This does not mean that these experiences themselves must be enjoyable but, after such a flow experience, we know that we have changed (Csikszentmihalyi, 1996).

Peak performances and other markers of experience

The literature that compares peak experiences and flow experiences is rich and is often joined by another category, peak performance, which is characterised not by the joy of experience but by superior functionality and excellent functioning (Privette, 1983). This includes such experiences in the natural environment and adventure activities with a certain degree of risk or uncertainty (Boniface, 2000). All three concepts overlap, where peak performance is characterised in particular by the full use of human potential in efficient, effective, creative and productive behaviour; it is a level of functionality, not an emotional attunement of pleasure or an internally rewarding, autotelic activity. For example, sports can be a good example of all three constructs of peak experience, peak performance and flow. However, listening to music can be a peak experience, but not a peak performance. Crisis moments in risky situations, such as a death threats, may be a stimulus for peak performance, but they are not a peak experience and are usually not flow. Inclusion in one of the three possible conceptual constructs may also be related to competitive orientation or mastery orientation, while athletes with a high mastery orientation are more likely to experience flow than athletes with a low level of orientation. At the same time, the flow experience is also associated with peak performance (Jackson and Roberts, 1992).

When attempting to search for a certain penetration, it is also possible to use the term 'peak moments', which links all three concepts into one concept with common characteristics: immersion in an activity or experience, spontaneous activity without awareness, emptiness and a loss of ego, euphoria and ecstasy, energy, an altered perception of time and the feeling of unity (McInman and Grove, 1991).

Another name for peak moments, especially in a sports environment, may also be 'being in the zone', which is closely related to spirituality (Dillon and Tait, 2000) and to a higher degree of bodily anchoring (Bednář, 2011).

Plateau experiences

In the last 15 months of his life, after a heart attack, Maslow suggested a paradigmatic turn; instead of focusing on self-actualised people with peak experiences, he discussed self-transcendence with plateau experiences (Gruel, 2015). Opposite from the towering peaks of the mountains with fleeting insight, the metaphor becomes a plateau, an upland of unifying consciousness of lifelong effort. This mode of experiencing differs from the emotionally exalted moments of peak experience or full passion in the state of flow. This mode is not so much about joy and fulfilment but rather about a peaceful and balanced state of deep understanding. While peak experiences can be purely emotional, without a noetic element, plateau experiences always contain a cognitive component. There is much more will and volition involved, so they become more like silent bliss than a peak explosion; they are less intense experiences of pure contemplative happiness that can be meaningfully attained. Unfortunately, this experiential mode has not been elaborated in detail; nevertheless, Maslow wanted to clarify: 'the tendency of some to identify experiences of transcendence as *only* dramatic, orgasmic, transient, "peaky", like a moment on the top of Mount Everest. There is also the high plateau, where one can *stay* "turned on"' (Maslow, 1994, p. XVI).

Holotropic experiences

The above examples of the analyses of experiences are an example of the change of focus in humanistic and positive psychology after a long period of interest in and concern with pathology, illness and dysfunction, the field began to re-focus on positive states, self-actualisation and personality-flourishing that enhance the quality of life, including happiness, creativity and transcendence (Seligman and Csikszentmihalyi, 2000). The last example, holotropic experience, is now a new branch of psychology.

Transpersonal psychology (Grof, 2008) extends the usual structure of human experiencing to a model that involves not only postnatal biography and individual consciousness but also – in connection with Jung's study of deeper psychic levels – birth events, perinatal states or even experiences beyond the individual contents of the psyche in areas of collective archetypes. This field in itself suggests that traditional psychology, based on strategies of verbal analysis, can expand into the direct expression of emotions and feelings that connect the mind to the body. There is, in fact, a renaissance of interest in Eastern spiritual currents, mystical traditions, transition rituals, rites of passage, ancient mysteries of death and the transcultural wisdom of primitive nations, including the methods of shamanism. These traditions accept extraordinary states of consciousness for which traditional science does not have adequate explanations. At the same time, such experiences may be healing, transformative, evolving and ontologically real, and they reveal the usual hidden dimension of existence in everydayness and are full of symbolic imagination and pictures.

The holotropic experience (holos = wholeness, trepein = moving towards something) has become the term to describe something that is directed or aimed at the whole because we identify with only a small part of what we are in ordinary consciousness. Such experiences can be induced by, for example, psychedelic substances, holotropic breathing, music and dance, sensory deprivation, spiritual therapy, etc. In such experiences, it is possible to transcend the narrow limits of the body and ego and encounter the rich spectrum of transpersonal experiences that help an individual to realise his or her full identity. There are experiential situations in which it is possible to extend the fragmentary experience of everyday life reflected in the ordinary state of consciousness to other dimensions of existence, with a high intensity of perception while simultaneously having no loss of full orientation in reality. These situations are usually accompanied by psychosomatic manifestations, and those who experience them strongly resist their negative characterisation as phantasms, or as imaginary. The unprejudiced study of this domain represents a real fundamental challenge not only for psychology but also for contemporary philosophy and science.

The beginnings of exploring holotropic experiences are related to the research with LSD and other psychedelics (Grof, 1972, 1977; Grof *et al.*, 2008). What matters most to us in this context is the fact that one encounter with such an experience can completely transform an individual's anchoring in the world to change his or her concept of human nature.

For example, a person who was raised an atheist and has a medical understanding of consciousness as a by-product of the brain, i.e. matter, can expand his perception of the world into a form of cosmic consciousness with all its creativity and variability after the first such experience. Holotropic experiences contribute to spiritual opening, the development of sympathy and tolerance, ecological sensitivity and a new order of values. It is not a consequence of religious indoctrination but of knowledge based on personal experience. However, the most interesting aspect is not the certainty of the people with such experiences, which observers may dismiss with an explanation of brain intoxication. The same experiences can be obtained without any substance or matter through a natural way of working with breath, evocative music and targeted body work (Grof and Grof, 2010). They can even appear spontaneously, without any apparent stimulus, and manifest themselves in the form of a psycho-spiritual crisis. Intensive experiential moments in an experiential education environment can also be a trigger for similarly exalted existential states.

Transformative experiences

Human experiences are variable and attempts to classify and organise them have been numerous. Some of the main definitions have been mentioned above, but this is not necessarily a complete listing. In addition to the aforementioned experiences, e.g. mindfulness, awe, mystical experiences and other experiences (Yaden *et al.*, 2017), the list of such 'trans-rational' human experiences have been posited as totalling more than 500 (Bednář, 2011).

However, for the purposes of this chapter, the joyful or delusional emotional state associated with these experiences is not important, whether it is experienced as pleasant, unpleasant or neutral, or whether it is characterised by transcendence or extraordinariness. Their transformative power is the potential of their pedagogical utilisation through experiential education. Therefore, the individual possibilities of the definition and terminology of the individual types of experiences (peak, flow, zone, nadir, plateau and holotropic) are reduced to our needs under the unifying name of transformative experiences.

Such transformative experiences can emerge in experiential education courses both spontaneously and through the dramaturgical arrangement of programmes into a meaningful wholeness, with the emphasis on concrete developmental goals. Both the peak experiences of full joy and fulfilment and holotropic states that exceed the rational readability of human understanding can emerge and appear, especially in nature-based activities. It is possible to feel such experiences while mountaineering, for example, given the fascination with mountain splendour, the exaggeration of oneself into spiritual dimensions of being, the imaginary flight through the airspace that accentuates the phenomenon of freedom, or the openness of the horizon with a new understanding of wholeness. Sea kayaking amazes one with the element of the sea and opens the sensitivity for life movement in the waves and the infinite vastness, splendour, astonishment over the wide horizontal planes of the surface and identification with the principles of depth and surfaces. Summer trips allow closer contact with plants and animals, and the night sky can overwhelm individuals with its endless depths and the stars' magical glitter. Winter camping conveys the power of contact with the ground, respect for frost and the desire to move the body to supply the necessary heat. Programmes that use group cohabitation rituals transfer a person across the boundaries of empathy and sharing. Extremely challenging movement games bring individuals to the limits of their strength and potential. Creative workshops can reveal the difference between what is and what might be. Discussion programmes make word limits problematic and create a desire for the richness of all forms and possibilities of interpersonal contact. In short, experiences in an experiential education framework make it possible to transform one's life with a desire for the holistic fulfilment of existence.

However, how does a rare event transform the whole of one's life? Individual uniqueness and the different contexts of human lives do not allow us to make such experiences mechanically in any way, or with an assumption of their general influence. For someone, a key point will be a fresh look at a large tree; for another person, it is a vibrant conversation founded in a deeply felt sharing of personalities. For yet another, it is joy from an unexpected victory in a game. However, a variety of experiences allows the possibility of transforming one's view of his/her own life up to a certain point to embark on a crossroads in a different direction than one would have chosen without such formative experiences. What enables life changes due to transformative experiences is the extension of the horizon, the shift of the context and meaningful understanding.

Experiential transformation of one's whole life

Horizon of experience

The concept of the horizon is familiar to everyone: it is a skyline that defines the range of what we can see, perceive and experience. We also all know from our own experience that the horizon is always present and that there is always an ultimate border of what limits our outlook, but we also know that the horizon can be changed. If we are surrounded by skyscrapers, our horizon is limited and restricted by nearby high-rise buildings. If we climb to the top of a high mountain, a completely different horizon opens before us that shows the wide-open landscape of the hills or mountains, depending on the peak from which we are looking. The horizon is therefore constant and variable. We cannot be rid of it, and we are always limited by it; but simultaneously, it offers a transformation that fundamentally influences the way that we perceive and experience ourselves. Moreover, we can help ourselves through targeted movement in the landscape to transform our experiences and their horizons.

The term 'horizon' is also conceived through phenomenological philosophy – that is, through texts that are not reader-friendly. Phenomenology is a method of removing all the thoughts that we have gained from years of social influence, whether it be school knowledge and understanding, value preferences of ideologies, prejudices, biases and distorted meanings. The problem is that we often accept these thoughts uncritically and unconditionally with the assumption of the real existence of the subject of such unverified knowledge. If we disregard this psychic content, we exclude them, we put them in brackets (*epoche*), and we can turn directly to what gives itself to us, to givens. The intentional focus of consciousness on the subject itself allows us to explore the form of experience itself. 'Experience' is therefore a basic category on which a strict phenomenological analysis is based and, within this framework, the concept of horizon is an extremely useful aid.

We focus on two authors from the rich literature who have somewhat different philosophical preferences, but for our purposes, we can present the basic delimitation that uses both sources. While Edmund Husserl expressed a preference for the analysis of consciousness and the problem of cognition, Jan Patočka prefers the topic of bodily anchoring in the world. However, they process the theme of the horizon in similar ways, as we observe in the following sections.

Husserl (1999) perceives the horizon as extended possibilities of actual experiencing and notifying. Our experiencing is characterised by undergoing a living presence, but with its focus and consciousness, it is only a part of the full meaning of experiencing reality. Beyond the boundaries of a particular experience, the indefinite open horizon spreads – the horizon of everything that is not directly experienced, but that partially participates in the constitution of the significance and meaning of the experience, and of what determines it. This open horizon is, for example, a past with all the possibilities of remembering earlier experiences and a future with a charged expectation of what is yet to come. However, in addition to temporality, there are also possibilities of everything that we can see right now, what we are able to focus on and what is beyond our current orientation – what stands some distance apart from our attention but what can potentially become our experience and is the background of the present experience. Therefore, every perception also includes what is not directly perceived but what is expected or remembered – the perceptual possibilities that could occur if we were to guide the perception differently. Even if new determinations do not come, these possibilities are open to the closer determination of purpose and of the meaning of the experience itself. Every experience in the process of the experiential stream has its horizon of references and indications, which significantly extend the possibilities of consciousness. 'The horizons are "predelineated" potentialities' (Husserl, 1999, p. 45). Within a given horizon, we can interpret and uncover a sense that is made clearer by explaining the newly awakened horizons. This openness creates the horizon of indications and references; moreover, the horizon itself is transformed, together with the conscious and unconscious connections of the experience itself. Therefore, our entire experience is endowed with a horizon structure.

For Patočka (1998), the horizon is also the skyline that encircles all items in the landscape and crosses it. The part of reality actually being experienced is always added to the assumed wholeness when the subject appears in different connections. Thus, every experience has relevance only in context, not in its isolation. However, a dynamically changing horizon, in which the movement of our corporality and our encounters with things is realised, can never be transferred to these things themselves. Experience is then related to the context of references that go beyond actuality itself – for example, the room is co-ordinated in other spatial contexts of a building, a street, a city, etc. This necessary incompleteness of our focus points to the horizon of all other possibilities – to the horizon of the in-actualities. We move with the centre of perceiving; therefore, our views change, but the horizon remains. Additionally, everything inside the horizon is determined by its relation to it, and the sense and the meaning of each individual item is co-determined by the horizon. 'Even a thing I ignore captures me in its horizons. (…) These horizons are not storehouses of memories as much as living fields which grasp us and lead us from experience to experience' (Patočka, 1998, p. 35). Everything appears to be in some horizon, which is a partly realised possibility; thus, the horizon widely extends the actuality of experiencing for living in possibilities. Our lives are concentrated on a certain opportunity, but other opportunities – which are not actual – remain part of a wider reference to the actually given. However, part of the horizon is not only consciousness but also a feeling, the inkling, the colouring of the atmosphere – all of this creates a horizon of reference and meaning: 'I is a horizon by its very nature' (Patočka, 1998, p. 59). The horizon of all reality, the horizon of horizons, is determined as a world in which everything is included. The world is a dynamically changing structure closely related to the transforming nature of our existence. 'Not perception, as for Husserl, but the factual movement of a bodily being constitutes the world for Patočka' (Blecha, 1995, p. 30).

Such an understanding of horizon has been studied and commented upon quite often. A large number of studies address this topic and seek delicate nuances in understanding (for example, Evink, 2013; Geniusas, 2012; Rabanaque, 2014; Walton, 2003, among others). Although we are open to using the idea of horizon in the analysis of an experience in the framework of experiential education, we must not forget the basic limits of rationality and conceptualisation, which were mentioned at the beginning of this chapter. Experience and horizons cannot be comprehensively and exhaustively conceptualised (Barber, 2008).

Widening of the horizon

The background of each phenomenon, including our particular experience, is therefore a horizon, which points to a whole of mutual relationships. Without the background of the horizon, we cannot perceive any individual item without a context, and a particular experience cannot be explicated.

> The horizon is somehow viewable, but it is not a thing. It is only an aspect of things in the world, seen or conceived from a certain point of view. The horizon of a thing changes also with the change of the viewpoint. Even the same thing can sometimes in other contexts show [to be] different.
>
> (Kratochvíl, 1994, p. 46)

How does the horizon relate to transformative experiences and experiential education? The intense experience I have through adventurous activities, being outdoors, wandering, etc. can change not only the meaning of the experience itself but also the horizon of my entire life through its transformational power. Similarly, because religious conversion shows the power of the moment by transforming all the values, references and meaning of the rest of one's life, the experience from an experiential education programme can offer a lifetime transformation. As an example, let us quote one participant's reflections from a course of snowshoeing and winter nature camping:

> The legacy of listening to my inner voice and living to the fullest in every moment accompanies me in my everyday life. I started doing things I had put off for a long time and for which I had not had enough

courage. (…) Searching for the meaning of my own life, which for me was one of the main themes [during the course], resulted in my deeper interest in the spiritual aspects of life.

(Jirásek and Svoboda, 2015, p. 85, 2016, p. 80)

Conclusion

In general terms, we can conclude that the significance of the concrete experiences that a participant can derive through activities and programmes in the discourse of experiential education does not lie in these experiences themselves. Their educational dimension can be seen through a category of transformative experiences that can be deliberately or spontaneously evoked through physical activities, the natural environment, the social atmosphere or other programmes commonly used in experiential education. Then, the transformation is related not only to an actual, presently experienced event but also to the entire horizon of references and meaning that extends the existing life directions to new, in-actualised possibilities. The change of the horizon of an entire life, in a long-term sense, can also be caused by a short-term experience, which has usually been studied in an isolated analysis. Linking the themes of transformative experiences and a lifelong horizon allows us to offer an answer to one of the most pressing issues in the field; it can be explained that even a short-term intervention in the form of an experiential course can transform the whole of human life from a long-term perspective.

Bibliography

Allen, R. M., Haupt, T. D. and Jones, R. W. 1964. Analysis of peak experiences reported by college students. *Journal of Clinical Psychology*, 20, 207–212.

Augustine 1966. *Confessions*, Washington, Catholic University of America Press.

Barber, M. D. 2008. Holism and horizon: Husserl and McDowell on non-conceptual content. *Husserl Studies*, 24, 79–97.

Bednář, M. 2011. Experiential gateway into spiritual dimension in sport. *Acta Facultatis Educationis Physicae Universitatis Comenianae*, 51, 75–84.

Blecha, I. 1995. *Jan Patočka a ohlas fenomenologie v české filosofii*, Olomouc, Vydavatelství Univerzity Palackého.

Boniface, M. R. 2000. Towards an understanding of flow and other positive experience phenomena within outdoor and adventurous activities. *Journal of Adventure Education and Outdoor Learning*, 1, 55–68.

Bottéro, J. 2001. *Religion in Ancient Mesopotamia*, Chicago, University of Chicago Press.

Breed, G. and Fagan, J. 1972. Religious dogmatism and peak experiences: A test of Maslow's hypothesis. *Psychological Reports*, 31, 866–866.

Corbin, H. 2007. *Mundus imaginalis, aneb Imaginární a imaginální*, Praha, Malvern.

Csikszentmihalyi, M. 1975a. *Beyond boredom and anxiety: Experiencing flow in work and play*, San Francisco, Jossey-Bass.

Csikszentmihalyi, M. 1975b. Play and intrinsic rewards. *Journal of Humanistic Psychology*, 15, 41–63.

Csikszentmihalyi, M. 1996. *O štěstí a smyslu života*, Praha, NLN – Nakladatelství Lidové noviny.

Dillon, K. M. and Tait, J. L. 2000. Spirituality and being in the zone in team sports: A relationships? *Journal of Sport Behavior*, 23, 91–100.

Dodson, K. J. 1996. Peak experiences and mountain biking: Incorporating the bike into the extended self. *Advances in Consumer Research*, 23, 317–322.

Eliade, M. 1959. *The sacred and the profane: the nature of religion*, New York, A Harvest Book (Harcourt, Brace and World, Inc.).

Eliade, M. 1971. *The myth of the eternal return: Cosmos and history*, Princeton, Princeton University Press.

Eliade, M. 1981. *History of religious ideas, volume 1: From the Stone Age to the Eleusinian mysteries*, Chicago, University of Chicago Press.

Evink, E. 2013. Horizons of expectation. Ricœur, Derrida, Patočka. *Studia Phaenomenologica*, 13, 297–323.

Fromm, E. 1956. *The art of loving*, New York, Harper and Row.

Geniusas, S. 2012. Introduction. *The origins of the Horizon in Husserl's phenomenology*, Springer, Dordrecht.

George, A. R. (trans.) 2003. *The epic of Gilgamesh: The Babylonian epic poem and other texts in Akkadian and Sumerian*, London, Penguin Books.

Grof, S. 1972. LSD and the cosmic game: Outline of psychedelic cosmology and ontology. *Journal for the Study of Consciousness*, 5, 165–193.

Grof, S. 1977. Perinatal roots of wars, totalitarianism, and revolutions: Observations from LSD research. *The Journal of Psychohistory*, 4, 269–308.

Grof, S. 2003. Implications of modern consciousness research for psychology: Holotropic experiences and their healing and heuristic potential. *The Humanistic Psychologist*, 31, 50–85.

Grof, S. 2008. Brief history of transpersonal psychology. *The International Journal of Transpersonal Studies*, 27, 46–54.

Grof, S. and Grof, C. 2010. *Holotropic breathwork: A new approach to self-exploration and therapy*, Albany, State University of New York Press.

Grof, S., Grob, C., Bravo, G. and Walsh, R. 2008. Birthing the transpersonal. *Journal of Transpersonal Psychology*, 40, 155–177.

Gruel, N. 2015. The plateau experience: An exploration of its origins, characteristics, and potential. *Journal of Transpersonal Psychology*, 47, 44–63.

Hallaq, J. H. 1977. Scaling and factor analyzing peak experiences. *Journal of Clinical Psychology*, 33, 77–82.

Haluza-Delay, R. 2000. Green fire and religious spirit. *Journal of Experiential Education*, 23, 143–49.

Heidegger, M. 2008. *Being and time*, New York, Harper & Row Publishers.

Heller, J. 1988. *Starověká náboženství*, Praha, Kalich.

Hitzhusen, G. E. 2004. Understanding the role of spirituality and theology in outdoor environmental education: A mixed method characterization of 12 Christian and Jewish outdoor programs. *Research in Outdoor Education*, 7, 39–56.

Husserl, E. 1999. *Cartesian meditations: An introduction to phenomenology*, Dordrecht, Kluwer Academic Publishers.

Jackson, S. A. and Roberts, G. C. 1992. Positive performance states of athletes: Toward a conceptual understanding of peak performance. *Sport Psychologist*, 6, 156–171.

Jaffé, A. 1989. *Memories, dreams, reflections – C. G. Jung*, New York, Vintage.

James, W. 1985. *The varieties of religious experience: a study in human nature*, New York, Penguin.

Jirásek, I. and Svoboda, J. 2015. *Putování a smysl života: proměna člověka v zimní přírodě*, Olomouc, Univerzita Palackého.

Jirásek, I. and Svoboda, J. 2016. *Non-religious peregrination and meaning of life: transformation of human being in winter nature*, Saarbrücken, Germany, Scholars' Press.

Jirásek, I., Veselský, P. and Poslt, J. 2017. Winter outdoor trekking: Spiritual aspects of environmental education. *Environmental Education Research*, 23, 1–22.

Jung, C. G. 1964. *Man and his symbols*, London, Aldus Books.

Kratochvíl, Z. 1994. *Filosofie živé přírody*, Praha, Herrmann a synové.

Kuhn, T. S. 1962. *The structure of scientific revolutions*, Chicago, University of Chicago Press.

Landsberg, P. L. 1990. *Zkušenost smrti*, Praha, Vyšehrad.

Margoshes, A. and Litt, S. 1966. Vivid experiences: Peak and nadir. *Journal of Clinical Psychology*, 22, 175–175.

Maslow, A. H. 1962. Lessons from the peak-experiences. *Journal of Humanistic Psychology*, 2, 9–18.

Maslow, A. H. 1994. *Religions, values, and peak-experiences*, New York, Penguin Books.

Maslow, A. H. 2011. *Toward a psychology of being*, Mansfield Centre, Martino Publishing.

McDonald, M. G., Wearing, S. and Ponting, J. 2009. The nature of peak experience in wilderness. *The Humanistic Psychologist*, 37, 370–385.

McInman, A. D. and Grove, J. R. 1991. Peak moments in sport: A literature review. *Quest*, 43, 333–351.

Michalson, J. D. 2005. *Ancient Greek religion*, Oxford, Blackwell Publishing.

Moody, R. 1975. *Life after life*, New York, Bantam.

Otto, R. 1958. *The idea of the holy: An inquiry into the non-rational factor in the idea of the divine and its relation to the rational*, New York, Oxford University Press.

Patočka, J. 1998. *Body, community, language, world*, Chicago, Open Court.

Plato 1997. *Complete works*, Indianopolis, Hackett Publishing Company.

Polyson, J. 1985. Students' peak experiences: A written exercise. *Teaching of Psychology*, 12, 211–213.

Privette, G. 1983. Peak experience, peak performance, and flow: A comparative analysis of positive human experiences. *Journal of Personality & Social Psychology*, 45, 1361–1368.

Rabanaque, L. R. 2014. Saulius Geniusas: The origins of the horizon in Husserl's phenomenology. *Husserl Studies*, 30, 187–194.

Ravizza, K. 1977. Peak experiences in sport. *Journal of Humanistic Psychology*, 17, 35–40.

Ring, K. and Cooper, S. 1997. Near-death and out-of-body experiences in the blind: A study of apparent eyeless vision. *Journal of Near-Death Studies*, 16, 101–147.

Seligman, M. E. and Csikszentmihalyi, M. 2000. Positive psychology: An introduction. *The American Psychologist*, 55, 5–14.

Sokol, J. 2004. *Člověk a náboženství: proměny vztahu člověka k posvátnému*, Praha, Portál.

Stringer, L. A. and McAvoy, L. H. 1992. The need for something different: Spirituality and wilderness adventure. *Journal of Experiential Education*, 15, 13–20.

Thorne, F. C. 1963. The clinical use of peak and nadir experience reports. *Journal of Clinical Psychology*, 19, 248–250.

Třísková, J. 1997. Německá a španělská mystika. *Problémy mysticismu: sborník příspěvků k buddhistické, islámské a křesťanské mystice*, Hradec Králové: Vysoká škola pedagogická, Fakulta pedagogická.

Walton, R. J. 2003. On the manifold senses of horizonedness. The theories of E. Husserl and A. Gurwitsch. *Husserl Studies*, 19, 1–24.

Yaden, D. B., Haidt, J., Hood, R. W., JR., Vago, D. R. and Newberg, A. B. 2017. The varieties of self-transcendent experience. *Review of General Psychology*, 21, 143–160.

Zuska, V. 1994. *Čas v možných světech obrazu: příspěvek k ontologii výtvarného uměleckého díla a procesu jeho recepce*, Praha, Univerzita Karlova.

Index

a priori 42, 63
academic 25, 78, 90, 92, 128
action 12, 38–9, 48, 56, 58–9, 61–3, 66–7, 70, 74, 82–3, 85, 115, 118
adjustment 93, 109
adventure 10–11, 16–17, 22, 25–9, 35–7, 90–4, 97–106, 109–12, 114, 118, 129; education 8, 13–14, 17, 25–2, 35, 90–1, 94, 106, 109–11; programming 8, 110; outdoor 4, 11, 17, 37, 93–4
aesthetic 4–5, 10, 20, 38, 41, 44–6, 50–1, 73, 82–8, 116–7; awareness 82; experience 5, 17, 44–5, 76–7, 83–5; feeling 38
Allison, P. 3, 5, 28, 30, 32–6, 72, 90–3, 96, 99, 106–11
Anglophone 2–3, 28–9, 31, 33, 35
Antarctica 29
anthropological 41, 68
apprehension 56–7, 59–60, 63, 66
Aristotelian 95
Aristotle 95
art 4, 14–15, 21, 37, 41, 44–7, 50–1, 76, 84, 89, 127; perception of 113
assertiveness 92
authentic 113

beauty 11, 41, 113, 116
behaviour 11, 48, 60–1, 63–4, 66, 92, 118
belief 32, 34, 87, 97, 115, 117
Berlin 30, 51
British Exploring Society (BES) 29
British Schools Exploring Society (BSES) 29

camping 2, 10, 12, 32, 99, 104–5, 108, 122, 125
canoeing 32, 91, 96, 98, 100–5
career 32, 73, 77, 87, 93, 95, 99, 102–3, 106–7
Cartesian 40, 69, 128
caving 32
character 3, 28, 34, 48, 60, 66, 74, 76, 79, 84, 95
civic 13, 15, 30, 45
climbing 24, 32, 118
cognition 38–9, 70, 123
cognitive 43, 47, 49, 67–8, 70, 84, 107, 114, 117, 119; attitude 39–40; value 39, 61
communication 44, 47, 56, 91
community 3, 8, 14, 20, 23, 32, 35, 39, 44, 47, 93–5, 97–8, 101–5, 107, 128; building 95
comprehension 56–7, 59, 66, 71, 84
conative 42–3, 46–7
conceptual 54–6, 58–9, 63, 65, 81, 88, 126, 128; ideas 72; interpretation 1, 56; perspective 10
confidence 92, 96, 99–101, 106–8
consciousness 37–41, 114–15, 118–21, 123–4, 127; individual 120; nature of 23–4; states of 112, 114, 120
consequence 39, 64, 66, 74–5, 84, 86, 115, 121
corporeal 60–3, 65
creative 3–4, 13–15, 17, 20, 37, 113, 116, 118, 122
Csikszentmihalyi, M. 6, 118, 120, 127, 129

cultural 2–3, 8–9, 12, 15, 20–1, 34, 44, 46–7, 49, 78, 109, 120
culture 8, 10, 12, 21, 45, 47, 51, 89, 93, 102–3, 113
curriculum 17, 33–4, 36, 71–2, 78–80, 82, 88–90; and pedagogy 78, 80

dance 116, 118, 120
Darwin, C. 80, 89
death 21, 29–30, 112–13, 118, 120, 129
deduction 58
deductive 94
delight 38
democracy 74, 79, 81, 89
desire 38, 97, 107, 113, 122
Dewey, J. 2, 5, 7, 9, 20, 28, 55, 71–90
dialectics 56–7, 59
Dilthey, W. 4, 37–43, 45–51
discipline 4–5, 9, 30, 33, 37, 40, 71, 86, 88
discourse 5, 12, 19, 71, 112, 114, 116, 126
dogmatism 58, 126
doing 54, 73–4, 76–9, 83, 86–8, 91, 125
dramaturgy 3, 14–15, 17
Drasdo, H. 34–5
Duke of Edinburgh Award 3, 28
Durham University 32

educative 72, 87, 89
effort and perseverance 97, 102–3, 106
embodiment 42, 48–9, 70
emotion 21, 23, 25, 39, 47, 76, 85, 93, 112
emotive 47, 76
empiricist 4, 38, 52–3, 59, 63, 65, 68
enjoyment 46, 76, 84
environment 12, 15, 21, 29, 48–9, 56, 62, 64, 74, 79–80, 91, 93, 99, 104–5, 107–8, 117–19, 121; natural 9, 117–18, 126; perceived 60; social 40, 48; sports 119
epistemological 4–5, 41, 52, 55, 57–9, 66–8
equality 22
erlebnis 4, 16, 37, 40, 49
ethical 33, 44, 49, 79, 87
existence 41, 43, 46–7, 49–50, 60, 83, 90, 113–14, 122–3, 125; dimensions of 120; habitual 63; human 47, 49
existential 42, 114, 121
expedition 4, 6, 22, 28–9, 33, 93–7, 99–111
expeditions 10, 13, 29–30, 34–5, 91–7, 106–9; influence of 5–6, 92–5, 97, 99, 107–9, 111; polar 22; school 96, 108–9; science 99; youth 5–6, 30, 91–2, 94, 108–9, 111
experiential 2–6, 13–21, 23, 35–6, 52–3, 55–61, 63–7, 69, 71–3, 89–90, 92, 109–15, 117, 120–2, 124–7, 129; course 112, 126; modes 56–8, 66–7, 114; moments 121; pedagogy 2, 8–9, 11, 13–15, 17, 112; situations 120

Faarlund, N. 3, 19–20, 23–5
faith 114–15
family 21, 39, 77, 99, 102–5, 117
fantasy 112–13
feeling 26, 38–40, 43–6, 48–9, 51, 99, 104–5, 108, 112, 116, 118–20, 124
flow 6, 37, 59, 114, 118–19, 121, 126–7, 129
Foglar, J. 2, 11
free 4, 12, 16, 21, 24, 31, 40, 89, 110
friendships 34, 93, 95, 97, 99, 102–3, 106–7
friluftsliv 3, 19–27

Galilean 40
Gestalt 41, 50, 55, 62, 67
Gestaltung 64
gesture 48
global 64, 66–7, 93, 95, 100–3
gratitude 97
growth 79–83, 86–7, 90–2, 102–3, 110
gymnasion 8, 12, 16–17

Hahn, K. 3, 28, 30–2, 35–6
Hegel, G.W.F. 26, 57, 74
historical 2–4, 32, 34, 37, 42, 45, 51, 53, 68
Hitler, A. 31
Hogan, J. 31
holistic 2–3, 11, 13–15, 17, 25, 61, 112–14, 122
holotropic 113–14, 119–21, 127

horizon 6–7, 41, 109–10, 112–15, 117, 119, 121–7, 129
humanistic 6, 113, 119, 127–9
Hume, D. 37
humility 33, 116
Husserl, E. 6, 49–51, 60, 68–9, 123–9
hylemorphic 53–4, 63, 65, 67

imagination 21, 31, 35, 40, 43, 45, 47, 50–1, 54, 85, 112–13, 115; creative 4, 37, 113; symbolic 120
impact 17, 79, 93, 99, 102–5, 109, 111
independence 92, 96, 100–3, 106
induction 58
inductive 94
intense 15, 107, 116–17, 119, 125
interaction 9, 34, 56, 58–9, 66, 76, 80, 87, 107
interpersonal 91–3, 99, 122
interrelation 56–7
interview 94–8
intimate 39, 72, 78, 88

James, W. 6, 31–2, 35, 55, 68, 115, 128
Jesus College Cambridge 32

Kant, I. 4–5, 37, 52–9, 63, 66–7, 69
Klouda, J. 4, 37–8, 40, 42, 44, 46, 48, 50, 68
knowing 37, 74, 77–80, 82–4, 86–8
knowledge 10, 23, 29, 37–8, 40, 52–3, 57, 66, 71–2, 78, 82–6, 88–90, 95, 99, 102–5, 108–10, 116, 121; content 5, 71; general 55; human 38; school 123; social 59–60; unverified 123
Kolb, D. 4–5, 20, 52, 55–60, 62–3, 66–9

landscape 10–11, 20–1, 23–4, 123–4
language 4, 8, 10–11, 15, 19–20, 38, 44, 47, 50, 64–5, 74, 102–3, 128
leadership 23, 109
Lederach, J.P. 35
Levick, M. 3, 28–30, 33, 35, 97
Lewin, K. 55
liberal 78
liberty 22
Locke, J. 37
locus of control 92
logical 5–6, 39, 55, 73–6, 84, 112

long-term 93, 95, 97, 99, 107, 109, 111
Longland, J. 3, 28, 32–5
love 11, 113, 115–17

MacDonald, R. 31
marriage 95, 107
Marshall, A. 6, 91, 94–7, 99, 106–7, 110
Maslow, A. 6, 113, 116–17, 119, 126, 128
meaning 6–9, 17, 19–21, 41, 44–8, 50, 54, 64, 69–70, 74, 76–7, 85–7, 109, 113, 116, 123–6, 128; constitution of 46; genesis of 45–6; interpretation of 21
mental 3, 16, 38, 43, 68, 78, 92, 106, 110, 112, 115–16
metaphor 45, 57, 115, 119
metaphysical 40–1
mindfulness 110, 121
mood 39, 44
moral 11, 22, 35, 49, 82, 90
Mortlock, C. 34, 36
motivation 59, 96
motor 61, 64, 68
Mountain Leadership Training Board 32
mountaineering 21, 96, 98, 100–5, 121
mountains 15, 21–2, 113, 116, 119, 123
mystical 6, 114–16, 120–1

nadir 6, 117, 121, 128–9
Nansen, F. 22, 26
nature 3, 6–7, 9–14, 17, 19–27, 33, 38–41, 44–9, 51, 71, 76, 84, 89, 99, 104–5, 107–8, 116–18, 120–1, 124–5, 127–8; developmental 118; human 38–40, 46–7, 49, 120, 128; indigenous 9; consciousness 23–4; protection 92
neugestaltung 64
normative 3, 41, 47, 50, 62, 64–5
Norwood Committee 31

observation 58–9, 61, 79
occupation 77–80, 82–3, 85–8
Operation Drake/Raleigh 30
Oslo 22–3, 25–7
outdoor education 2–5, 8, 12–17, 28–36, 71, 77, 88–90, 109, 128

Outward Bound 3, 13, 15, 28, 31–2, 34–5, 93, 110

paradigm 95, 100–1, 112
parenthood 95
Parry, S.J. 2, 4, 6
pathology 62, 119
peacebuilding 34–5
pedagogy 2–3, 5, 8–9, 11, 13–17, 19–20, 70–2, 89, 112–14; curriculum and 78, 80
Peirce, C.S. 67, 69, 74, 90
perception 4, 21, 37–8, 41–2, 46, 48–50, 57, 60–3, 65–70, 76, 94, 112–13, 119–21, 124–5; altered 119; of art 113; of beauty 116; intensity of 120; visual 68
perceptual 39, 44, 59–62, 68, 124
personal 11–12, 33, 42, 47–9, 56, 60, 67, 74, 84–5, 87, 89, 91–3, 95–6, 100–3, 109–11, 115, 121; accountability 95, 100–1, 106; development 9, 29, 92, 106–7, 111; growth 102–3, 110; identity 95
Personal Social and Health Education (PSHE) 33
personality 22, 33, 92, 120, 122, 129
Peters, R.S. 5, 7, 73–5, 78–90
phenomena 9, 20, 39, 45–6, 54, 62, 126
phenomenalism 39
phenomenological 41, 50–1, 60, 66, 94, 123
phenomenology 2, 5, 52, 60, 68–70, 123, 128–9
philosophical 9, 21, 23, 37–40, 42, 49–50, 52, 70, 88–9, 112–14; approach 4; background 4, 37; heritage 4, 37; preferences 123; reflections 112; tradition 38–9, 113; understanding 6, 114
physical 10, 14–16, 33–4, 48–9, 61, 67, 83, 96–7, 99–101, 106–7, 117, 126; challenge 21; condition 39; education 8, 12, 19, 70, 96; movement 3, 14–5; nature 48; skills 92; training 97
Piaget, J. 17, 55, 67
planning and preparation 96, 104–5, 108–9

Plato 31, 52–3, 56, 67–9, 113, 128
play 3–4, 11, 13, 15, 20–1, 26, 37, 53, 56, 63–4, 76, 79, 86, 127
poetics 4, 37, 39–41, 45–7, 49–50
potential 14–15, 44, 64, 67, 97, 99–101, 112–13, 116, 118, 121–2, 124, 127; formative 49; identify 97; realising 92, 106; transformational 112; transformative 6, 112
practice 2–6, 8–9, 13, 16, 19–21, 23–5, 28, 32, 34–6, 67, 69, 71–2, 77, 86–8, 90, 94–5, 100–2, 106, 108–10; future 6, 109; pedagogical 5, 19–20; teaching 71; theory and 74, 88, 110
pragmatic 58, 74, 84, 88
Prague 12, 69
Pring, R. 73, 80, 90
psyche 41, 113, 120
psychic 41–7, 50, 120, 123
psychological 6, 14–15, 37, 41, 50, 58, 72, 112, 114, 126
psychology 41, 46, 50, 55, 67–8, 78, 113–14, 119–20, 126–9
Public Schools Exploring Society (PSES) 29

Quay, J. 5, 9, 17, 71–2, 74, 76–8, 80, 82, 84, 86, 88, 90

Ramirez, M-J. 5, 91–2, 94, 96–7, 99, 106–10
reflection 8, 14, 20, 23, 56, 58–9, 75, 85, 89, 93, 99, 102–3, 106, 112–14, 125, 128; pedagogical 114; theoretical 2
relationship 9, 11, 32, 65, 81, 93, 99, 102–3, 106, 125, 127; balanced 13; caring 113
religion 46, 114–15, 126–8
religious 6, 17, 39, 50, 82, 113–17, 121, 125–8
resilience 92, 99–101, 110
responsibility 24, 79, 97, 102–3
Round Square Schools 3, 28, 32

safety 13, 23–4, 34
sailing 94, 98–105
Salem School 30–1
scepticism 57–8
schemata 47, 68

science 4–5, 11, 22, 25–7, 29, 35, 37, 40–1, 44, 46, 51, 67–71, 82, 85, 89, 97–105, 110, 112–5; natural 11; philosophy and 120; religious 114; traditional 120; western 112
Scott, R.F. 29, 35
sea 93, 116, 122
Seifert, M. 11, 18
sensibility 53–4, 56
sensory 54–5, 63–4, 113, 120
service 6, 32, 35, 87, 94, 97–8, 104–5, 108, 110
seton 11, 18
Shackleton, E. 29
significance 42, 61, 86, 95, 100–1, 106, 110, 123, 126
skills 10–11, 14, 20, 23, 64, 92–5, 97, 99–106, 108, 111, 117–8; collaborative 93; corporeal 60; habits and 95, 106; interpersonal 93; motor 64; outdoor 99, 104–5
Social Emotional and Ethical Learning (SEEL) 33
somatic 42
spiritual 30, 48, 113, 115–17, 120–2, 126, 128
sports 8, 10, 12–13, 32, 116–19, 127
stereotype 47
Stott, T.S. 5, 30, 35, 91–4, 106, 109, 111
subject 16, 33, 37, 39–40, 49, 53, 56, 60–2, 69–71, 78, 82, 84–6, 88, 114, 123–4
subjectivity 40, 44, 69
summer 10–11, 14, 16, 21, 122
symbolic 4, 37, 44, 56, 59, 113, 120

teach 25
Terra Nova Expedition 28–9
thematic analysis 92, 96–7, 106, 111
themes 6, 34, 69, 94–7, 106, 126

thinking 24, 38, 45–6, 59, 64, 68, 70, 72, 74–5, 80; complex 107; environmental 19; rational 115; reflective 74, 89; theoretical 45
transaction 56–9, 67
transcendence 119–21
transcendental 54, 68, 116
transformative 6, 112–15, 117, 119–23, 125–7, 129
transformed 10, 42–3, 112, 124
transpersonal 113, 120, 127
trekking 15, 98–9, 108, 128
turistika 2, 8–10, 15–17

United World Colleges 3, 28, 32
University of Edinburgh 110

Vacation School of Lipnice 8, 9, 13, 14, 15
validity 58
value 6, 10–11, 19, 22–3, 25, 39, 52, 60–2, 67, 81, 84, 89, 93–5, 99, 102–3, 106, 109, 113, 115, 121, 123, 125, 128
Values clarification 95, 102–3
vegleder 24–5
vegledning 3, 19–21, 23–5
virtue 22, 94–5, 100–1
vivid 117, 128
volitional 38–9, 114
volunteer 15
Vygotsky, L. 20

White Hall 32–5
wilderness 23, 29, 91, 107–11, 128–9
winter 14, 17, 35, 69, 122, 125, 128
woodcraft 2, 9–12, 18

Yorkshire Schools Exploring Society (YSES) 30

Ingram Content Group UK Ltd.
Milton Keynes UK
UKHW021306020723
424425UK00021B/735

9 780367 787790